MW01631031

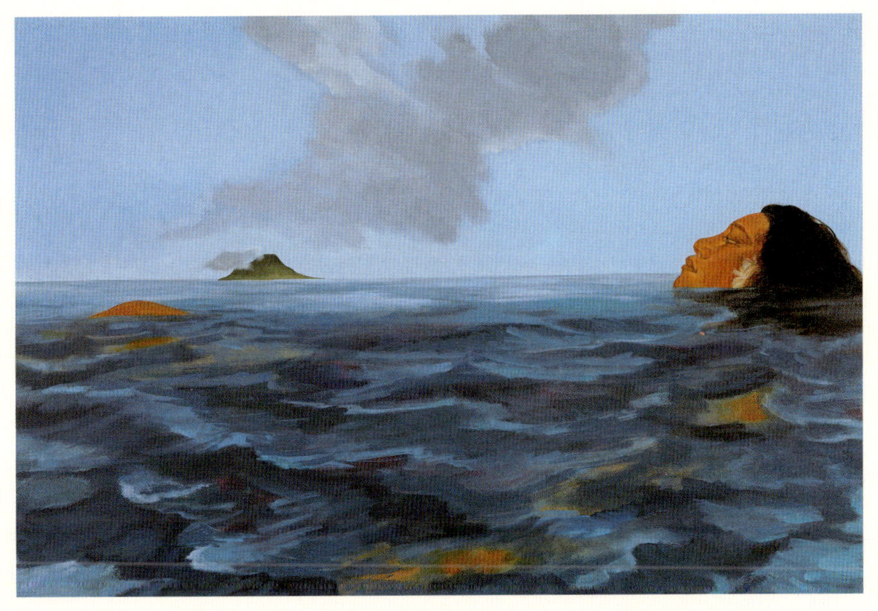

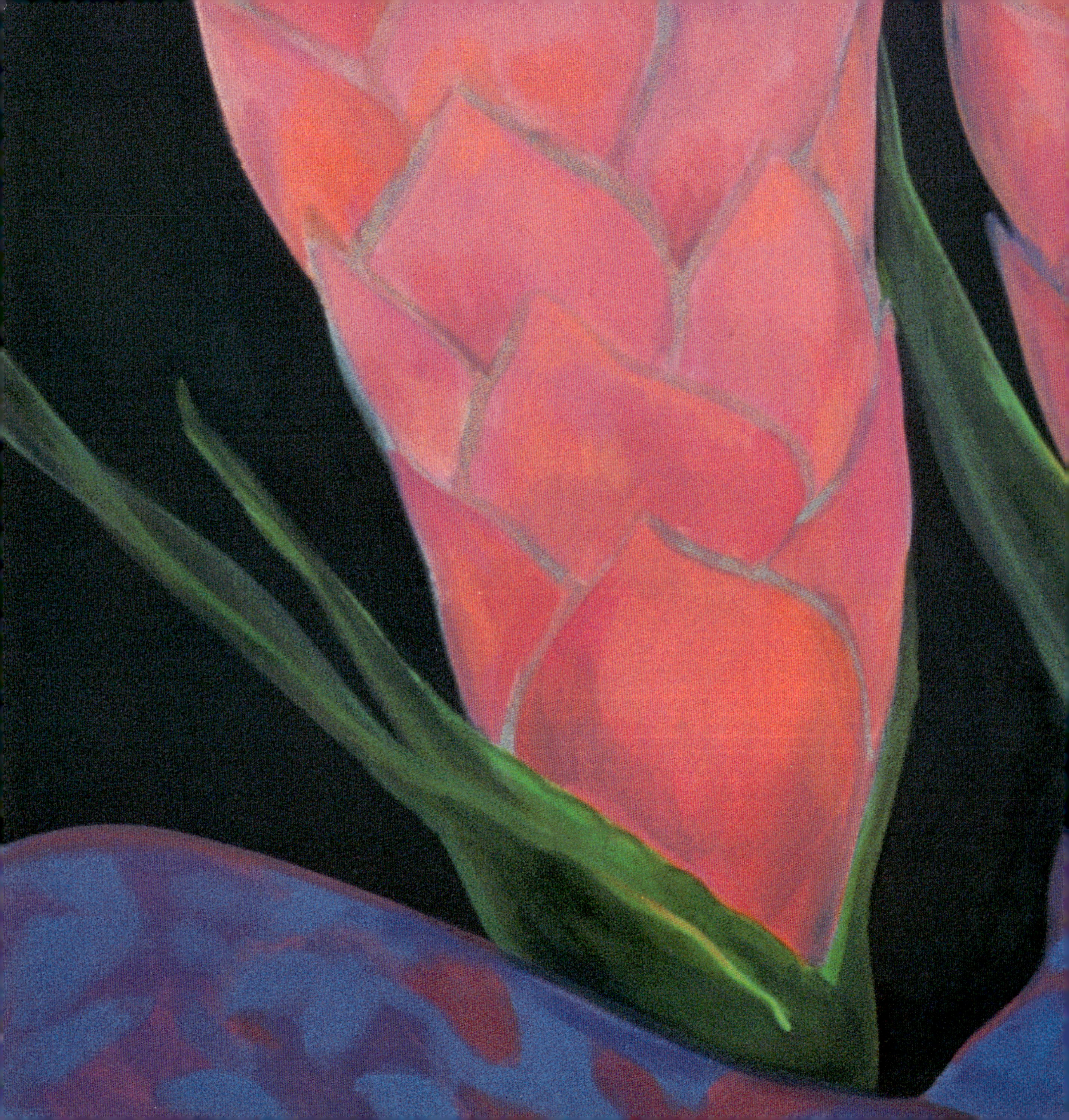

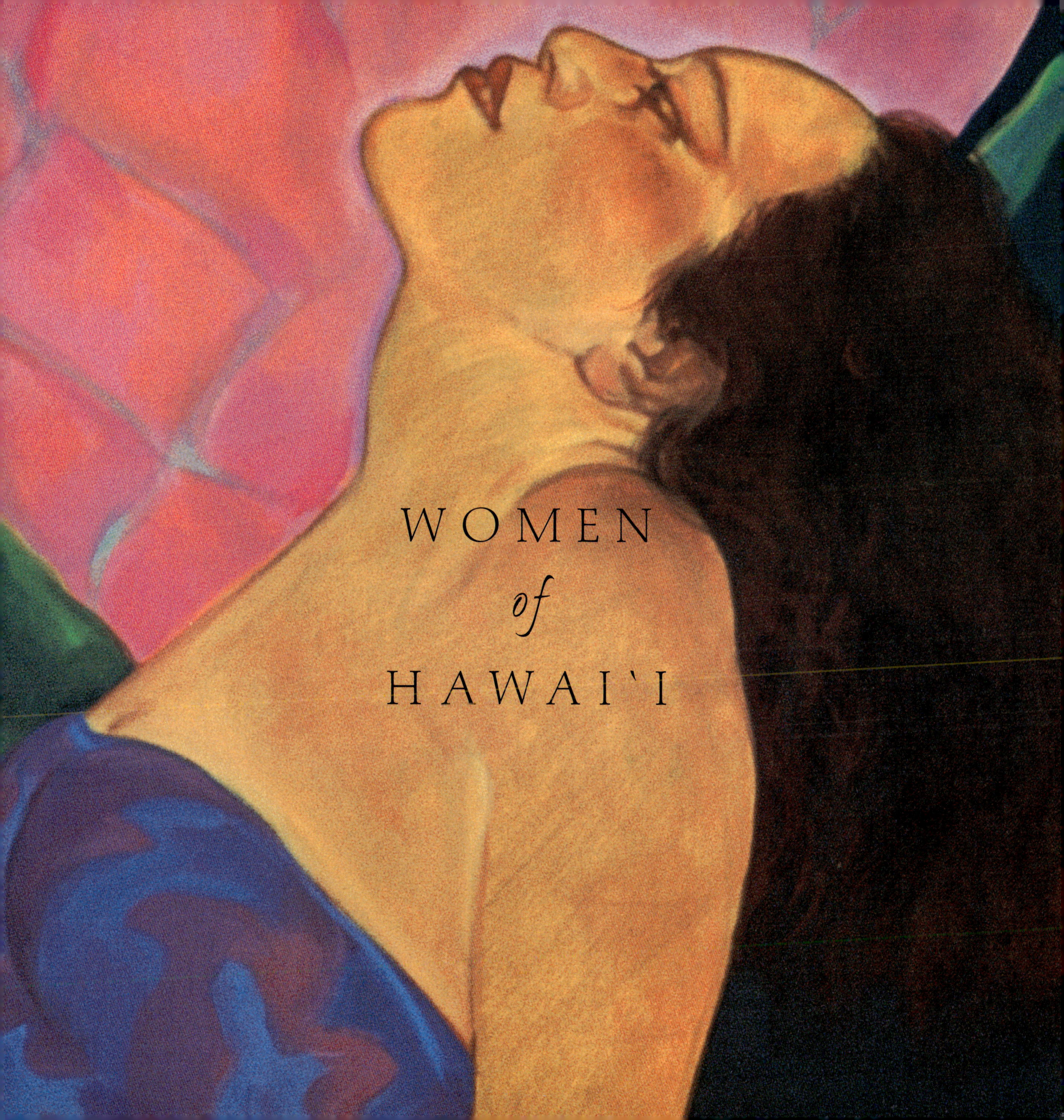

WOMEN *of* HAWAI'I

WOMEN *of* HAWAI'I

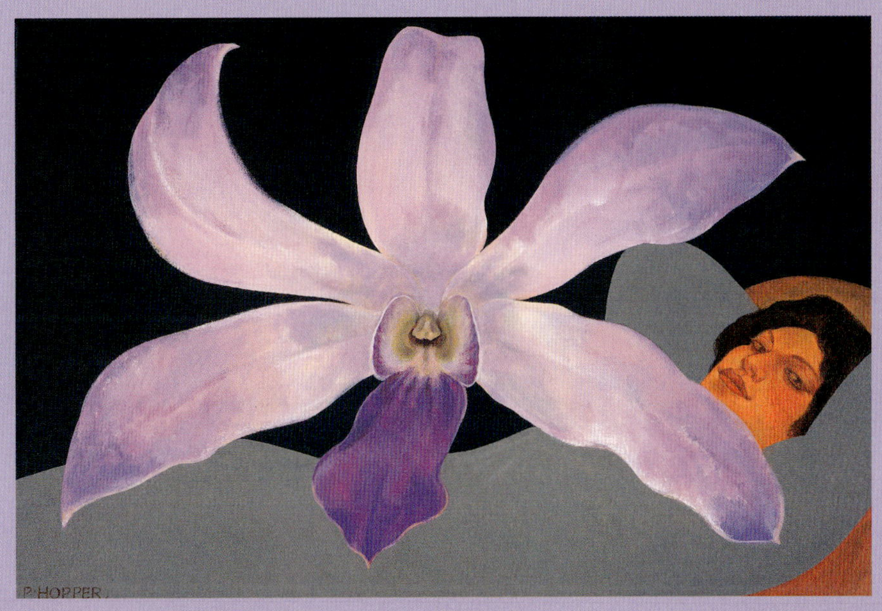

PEGGE HOPPER

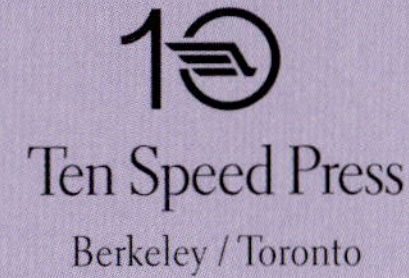

Ten Speed Press
Berkeley / Toronto

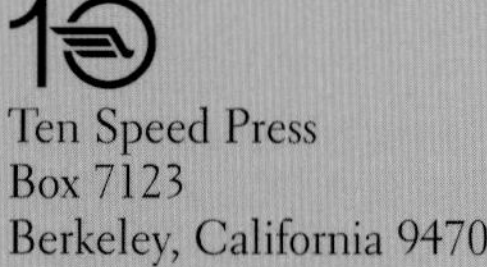

Ten Speed Press
Box 7123
Berkeley, California 94707
www.tenspeed.com

Distributed in Australia by Simon & Schuster Australia, in Canada by Ten Speed Press Canada, in New Zealand by Southern Publishers Group, in South Africa by Real Books, in Southeast Asia by Berkeley Books, and in the United Kingdom and Europe by Airlift Book Company.

Cover and text design by Jeff Puda

Library of Congress Cataloging-in-Publication Data on file with the publisher.

Printed in Korea

1 2 3 4 5 6 7 8 9 10 — 06 05 04 03 02

page i: *Untitled*, acrylic on canvas, 1989
pages ii–iii: *Akala Wahine*, acrylic on canvas, 2000
page v: *Okika*, acrylic on canvas, 2000

INTRODUCTION

I was very young when I realized that drawing was what I really loved to do. I never did well academically; I had trouble following directions closely and it seemed that I was never properly prepared for tests. I never felt like I fit in and I wasn't comfortable with the social scene. I don't think my parents were pleased when I chose to go to art school rather than college, but it was my mother who encouraged me to go to a commercial school instead of a fine arts school so I could, as she said, "support myself, if necessary." Since my family was living in Southern California when I finished high school, I enrolled at the Los Angeles Art Center, now called the Art Center College of Design, in Pasadena, in 1953.

I took courses in painting, illustration, lettering, and advertising art during my seven semesters at Art Center. It was competitive and stimulating and I felt like I finally belonged. The teachers were excellent and the students were dedicated. Many of my classmates were returning Korean War veterans and they were serious about preparing for their art careers. They set a tone of hard work and study. When I wasn't in school, I was at home in the garage trying to paint like El Greco and Cézanne.

During this time, my mother became ill with cancer. Watching my mother suffer from a painful illness was a sobering experience. I left school for a semester and helped care for her until she died. I was nineteen years old and my mother's death devastated me. It forced me to confront one of life's cruel realities at an early age, and I needed to get away. Rather than return to Art Center, I wanted to go to the American School in Rome or the Instituto Allende in San Miguel de Allende, Mexico. At my father's insistence, I returned to Art Center and prepared a portfolio.

{OPPOSITE TOP} *Untitled*
36 x 20 inches, oil on board, 1954
Collection of the artist

{OPPOSITE BOTTOM} *Untitled*
29 x 24 inches, oil on board, 1955
Collection of the artist

My career as a professional artist began in New York City. Two girlfriends who had just graduated from the Art Center were going to New York to look for jobs. By this time I had completed a portfolio, and I wanted to go with them. My father made a trip to the Art Center to talk to my teachers to see if I really had talent. He had to be sure I was going to succeed and wouldn't end up starving in a garret. My teachers assured him I was going to do fine, so he let me go. I remember he paid $99 for the plane ticket.

New York didn't intimidate me, I think because I was sure I had received a good education. I felt good about my portfolio, and I knew I could depend on myself to work hard. I tramped around town looking for a job wearing my high heels and white gloves and carrying my heavy portfolio. It was the summer of 1956 and I was twenty-one years old. I was offered a job at Raymond Loewy Associates, an industrial design firm, and even though I really wanted to work for a magazine as an illustrator, I accepted the job. Mr. Loewy was French, a real gentleman, and always impeccably dressed and courteous. I worked in the interior design department, which at the time was providing interior murals for major department stores. I learned a lot from the other designers with whom I worked.

I worked for Mr. Loewy for about a year. While there, I met my future husband, Bruce, a graphic designer. We married in 1957 and moved to San Francisco. In 1960, we moved to New Canaan, Connecticut, so my husband could work with the well-known designer Eliot Noyes. During the years we lived in San Francisco and New Canaan, I worked with Bruce on his graphic design projects and did a little freelancing.

In late 1960, we decided to go to Europe. After traveling and living in our VW van for four months, we decided we'd better look for jobs. We took our portfolios to La Rinascente, a big department store in Milan. It was a prestigious chain, like Neiman-Marcus or Bloomingdale's. They did fabulous graphic work, and they hired us. We were there for two years, and that's when I started to take myself seriously as an artist. I was given a lot of responsibility and did some good work, mostly posters. I believe that's when my style began to develop.

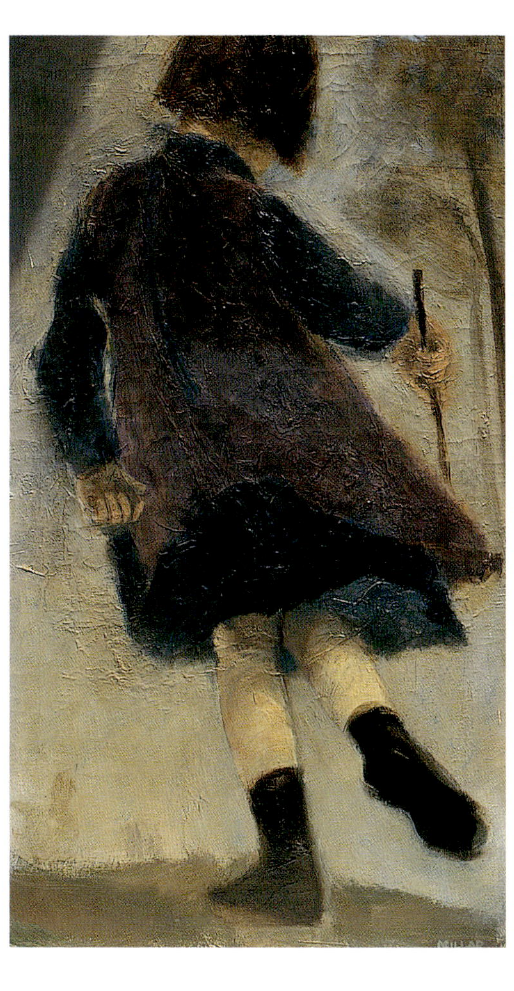

3

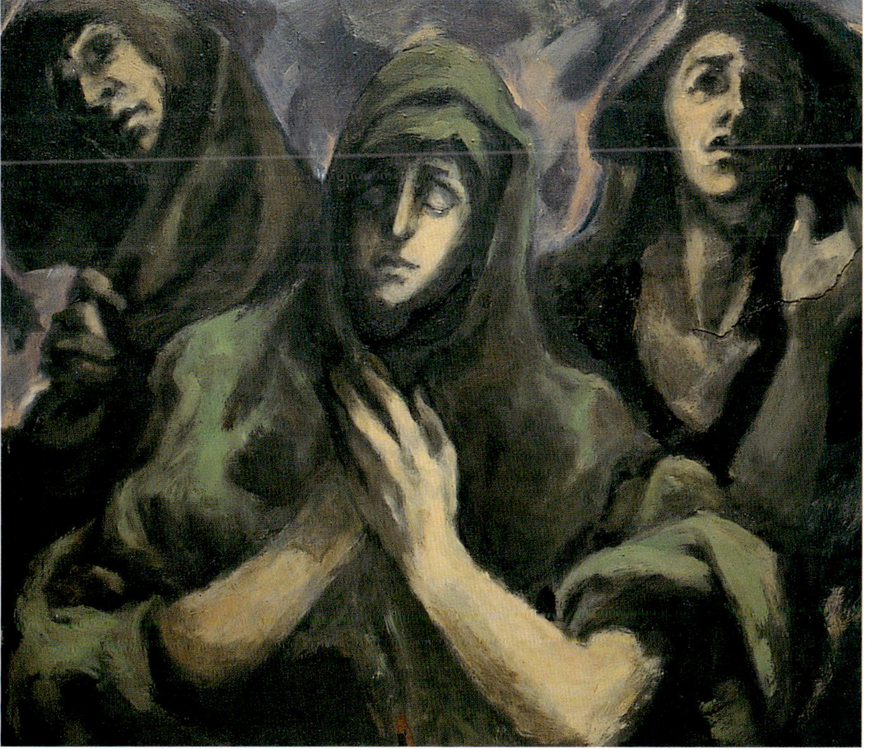

At La Rinascente I had replaced a Swiss designer who had set a tone of excellence that I felt I had to either meet or surpass. I was doing institutional art as opposed to merchandising or advertising layout work. I began to combine my drawing skills with flat graphic design and I loved it. For those two years in Milan I was on top of the world. However, a desire to start a family brought us back to the United States. Though our daughter Allison was born in Los Angeles and our original intent was to stay there, the smog, traffic, and expansive size sent us searching for a new home. That search brought us to Hawai`i.

Hawai`i was a long way from Oakland, California, where I was born, and it was very different from any place I had ever lived. Everything seemed so young and innocent, so new and fresh, so vibrant and lushly organic, especially compared to the ancient buildings, old-world art and culture, and design sophistication we had just recently left in Milan. We didn't know *anybody* here. While Bruce worked hard to establish a graphic design business, I worked as an art director at an advertising agency and took care of the children. (Jennifer was born in 1965 and Lauren followed in 1976.)

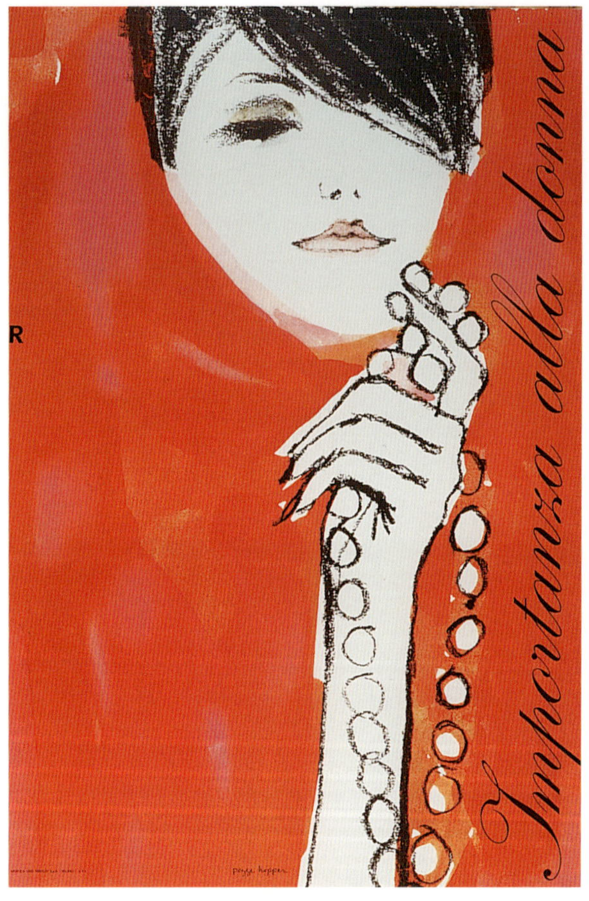

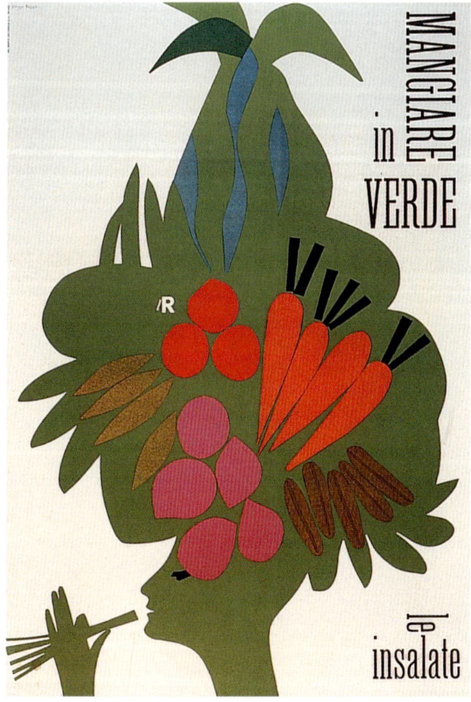

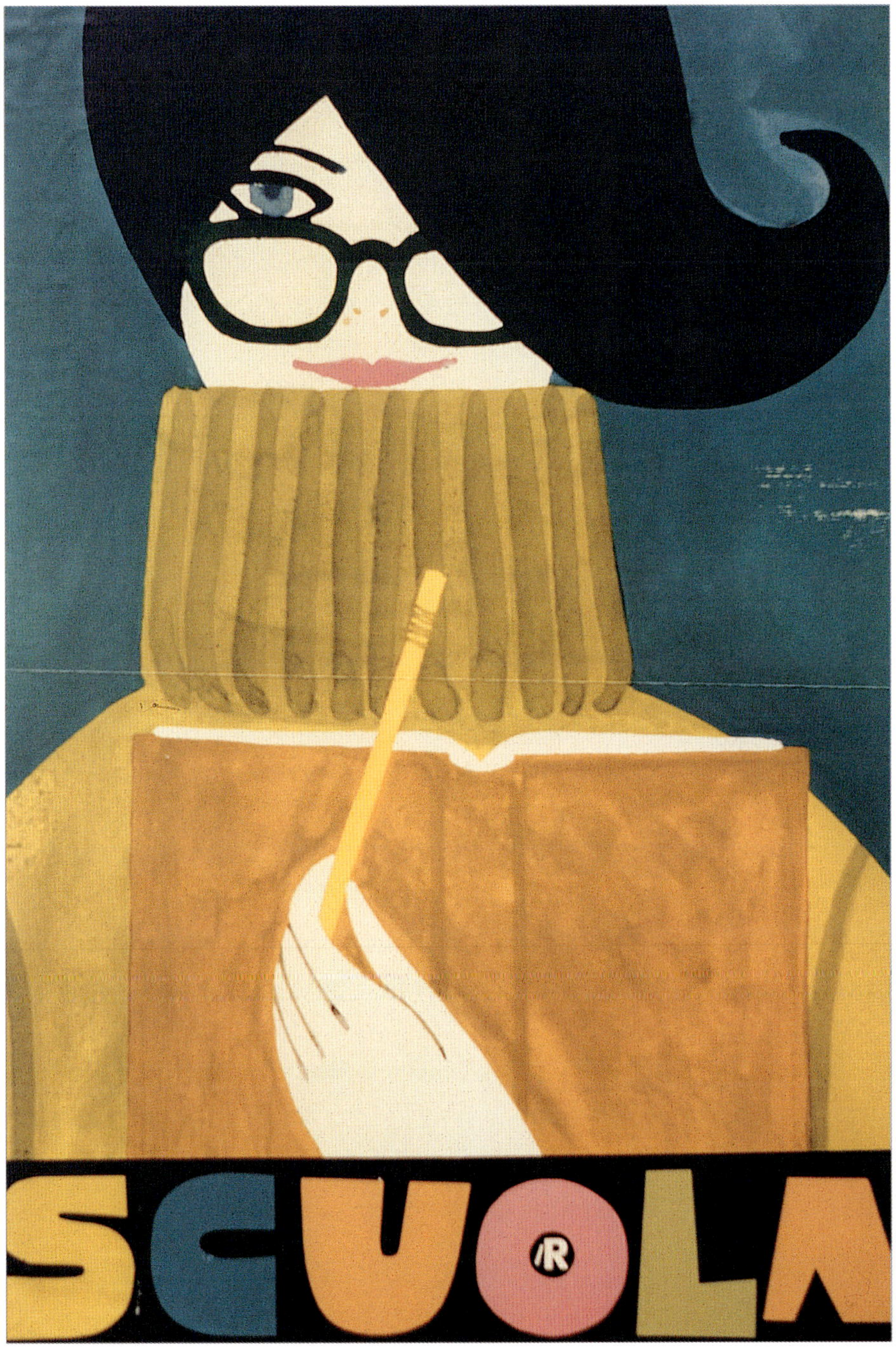

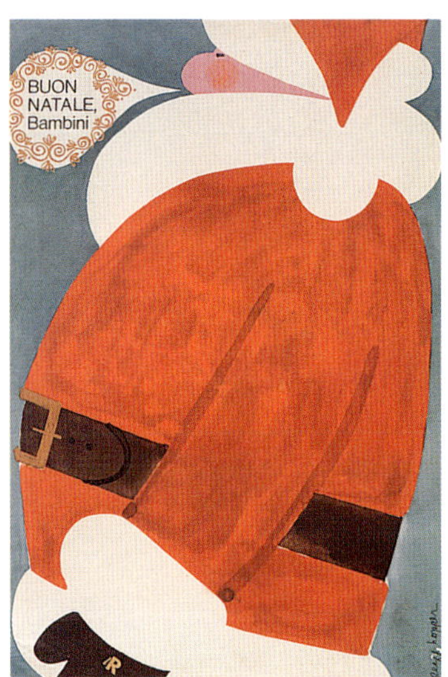

Posters
30 x 40 inches, offset lithographs, 1962–63
La Rinascente, Milan

{OPPOSITE} *Lauren and Elly*
3 x 4 feet, acrylic on board, 1997
Pegge Hopper Gallery, Honolulu

Lauren
4 x 4 feet, charcoal and acrylic on board, 1993
Private collection

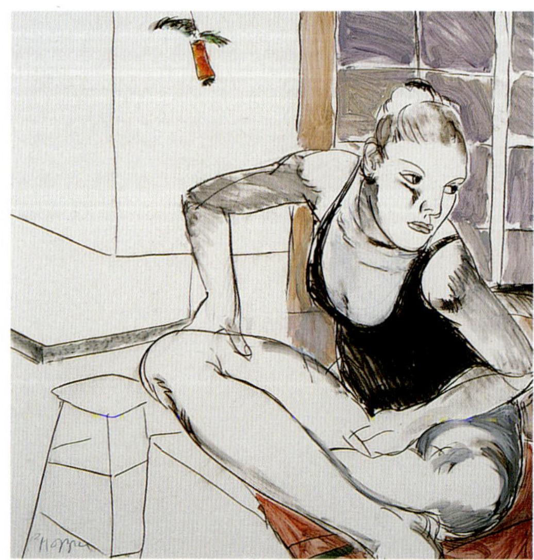

Family life kept us busy and weekends were spent fixing up an old house that we had bought in Nuuanu in 1968. It was during this period that I began to visit the state archives to study old photographs. I was intrigued by the faces of the Polynesian people. Their open and unself-conscious gazes stared at me from another era, and whether in their native clothing or stuffed into Victorian nipped-waist dresses, I was inspired to paint them.

My first paintings were sketchy and rough, but they attracted the attention of my friend, Mary Philpotts, an interior designer. She told me she was doing a renovation at the Kona Village on the Big Island and asked me to do twenty-two paintings. By then I had left the ad agency, so Mary's timing was perfect. My career as a painter was launched—and I never looked back.

Since that first commission in 1969, more commissions and gallery shows followed. I was honored when the Bishop Museum in Honolulu selected me to design their annual poster. That recognition, along with my relationships with other island charities, exposed my work to a wider audience and gave me a chance to be involved in the community.

The demand for my commissioned originals encouraged me to pursue an idea I had to produce prints and posters of my work as a business venture. My first experience creating serigraphs started out on Sand Island Road in a sign-maker's shop, where signs such as "No Parking" were printed. My husband had taken a screen-printing class in high school, so he knew something about the process. It was a makeshift, jury-rigged sort of operation. Termites would be flying around the shop and falling into the ink. We'd get an edition of about 120 out of 300 sheets of paper. The mortality rate was incredible and I still use a lot of the spoils from those early efforts for scratch paper. But the serigraphs sold well, and that encouraged us to keep going.

In 1981, my serigraphs and posters caught the eye of Larry Winn, a mainland publisher of fine art prints. He wanted to publish and distribute the serigraphs and to make available to me the sophisticated printing facilities of his organization. He made an offer that I couldn't refuse. He treated me fairly and always had respect for my work. He helped me understand how to combine

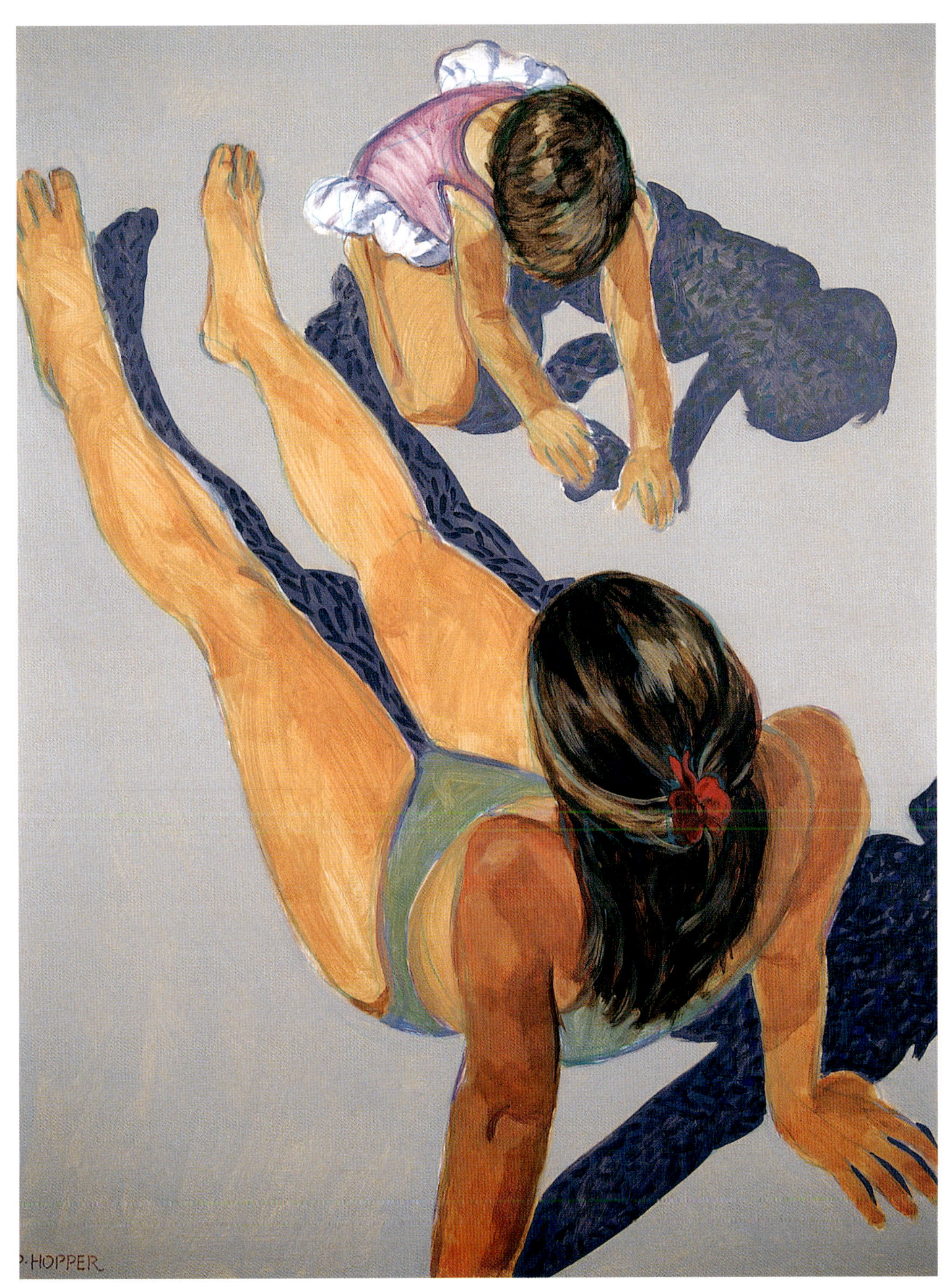
P. HOPPER

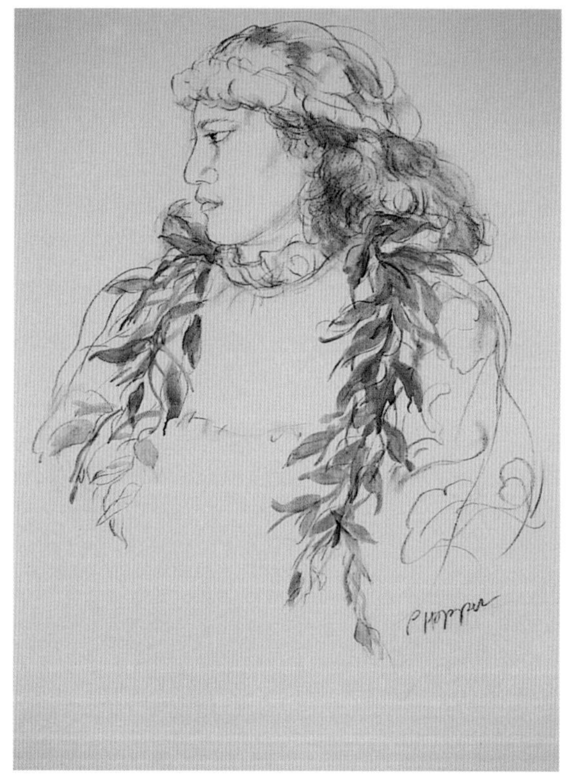

business and art, and as a consequence of our business relationship, my work began to get widespread distribution outside the Hawaiian Islands.

Though we had purchased our home in Nuuanu in 1968, I didn't add a studio until 1980. Moving out of the house into my own workspace made me feel like a real artist. In 1983, I rented an interesting, old building in historic Chinatown and opened my own gallery. I rode the wave of the exploding art market during the eighties and early nineties, and my popularity as an artist exceeded my wildest dreams. In 1986, a building next door to my gallery came on the market, and I bought and renovated the property where my gallery is located today. It was this project that whetted my appetite for architecture.

In 1990, I purchased a home in San Miguel de Allende, Mexico, a place that is very supportive of artists and that had intrigued me for many years. I renovated a property in the beautiful, colonial El Centro, fulfilling my old dream of living in San Miguel and also satisfying an urge to create my own space. With my lack of architectural experience and inability to speak Spanish, it took a long time to complete the remodel, but in 1995 my home in Mexico was finished.

I have drawn inspiration from the culture of the Mexican people, and I find a similarity between the Polynesian women's faces and those of the Mexican women. I studied photographs taken during the 1910 Mexican Revolution with the same interest that I viewed the archived photographs of Hawaiian women taken during approximately the same era. The women's strong, expressive faces say so much about both suffering and competence; a contrast to the stereotyped images of women that our culture seems to revere today.

When I first started to paint Hawaiian women I felt they had not yet been depicted in a contemporary style. So I used my drawing skills in combination with graphic imagery to portray the fortitude and some of the sadness that I had seen in the old photographs. I don't paint from my head, I paint from my eyes, and although I don't know many Hawaiian women personally, their beauty has become etched in my mind. I know them from the outside only, and have never dared to invade their privacy.

Today I am in the process of building a new house from the ground up. I hope it will turn out just as I imagine it—a simple, serene home in which to create and grow old. My family is grown and my three daughters are on their own, but I have two little granddaughters who bring me great joy. Since I have lived in Honolulu for more than half my life, I feel like a *kama`aina* in spirit. I realize how fortunate I am and how much support this community has given me, both as an artist and as a woman. I hope that through my art I have given something back.

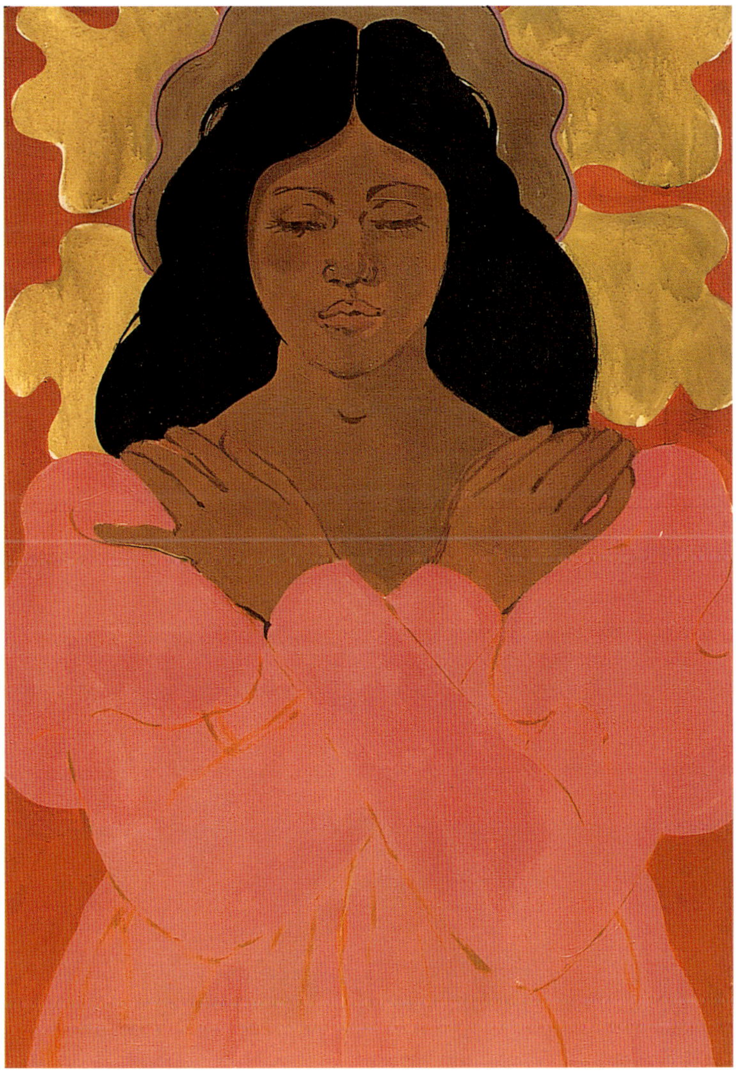

{OPPOSITE} *Untitled*
30 x 40 inches, charcoal on canvas, 2002
Pegge Hopper Gallery, Honolulu

Untitled
39 x 27 inches, acrylic on canvas, 1968
Collection of the artist (My first painting of a Hawaiian woman)

Pele

10 4 x 5 feet, acrylic on canvas, circa 1990
Private collection

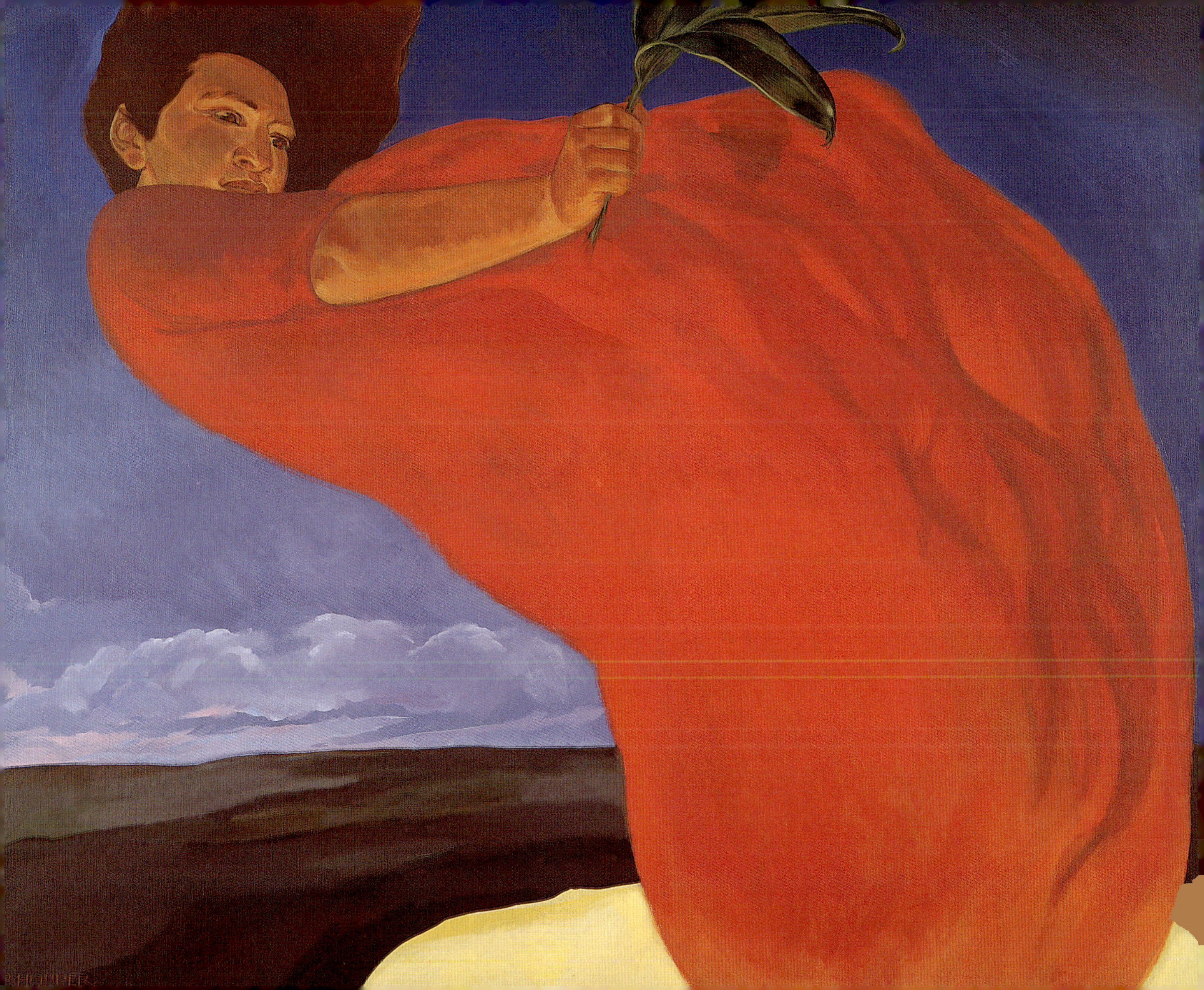

Bromiliad

12 2 x 3 feet, acrylic on canvas, 1999
Napua Gallery, Maui

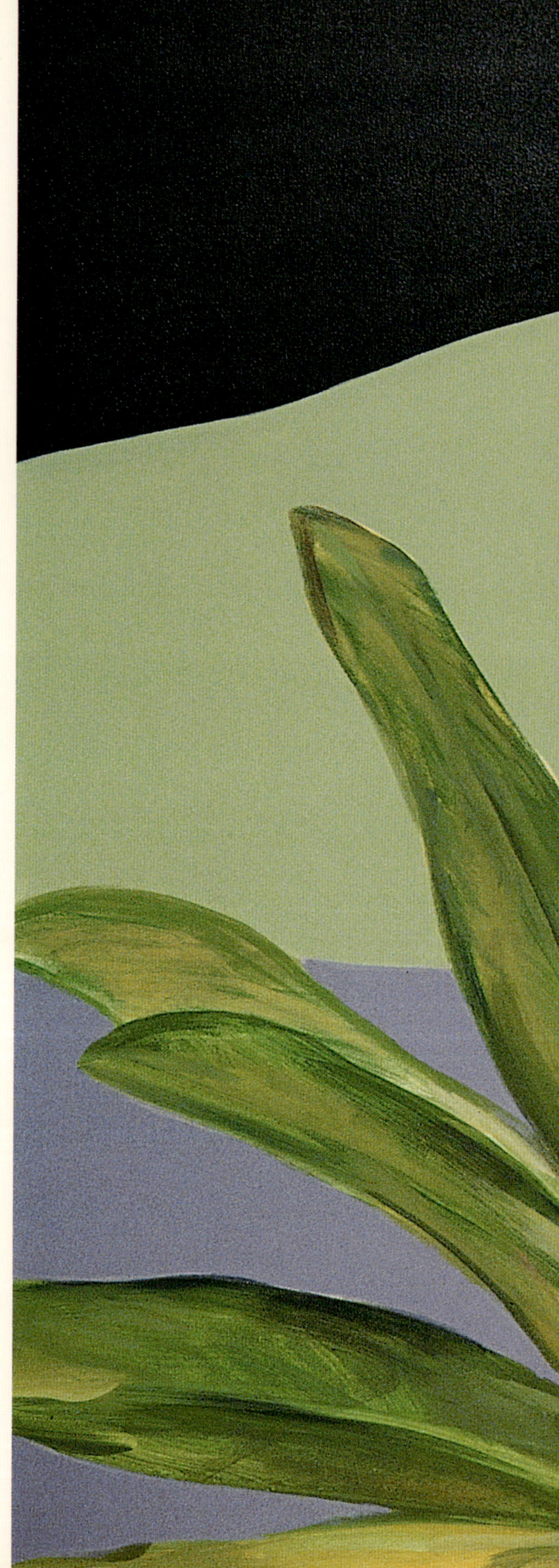

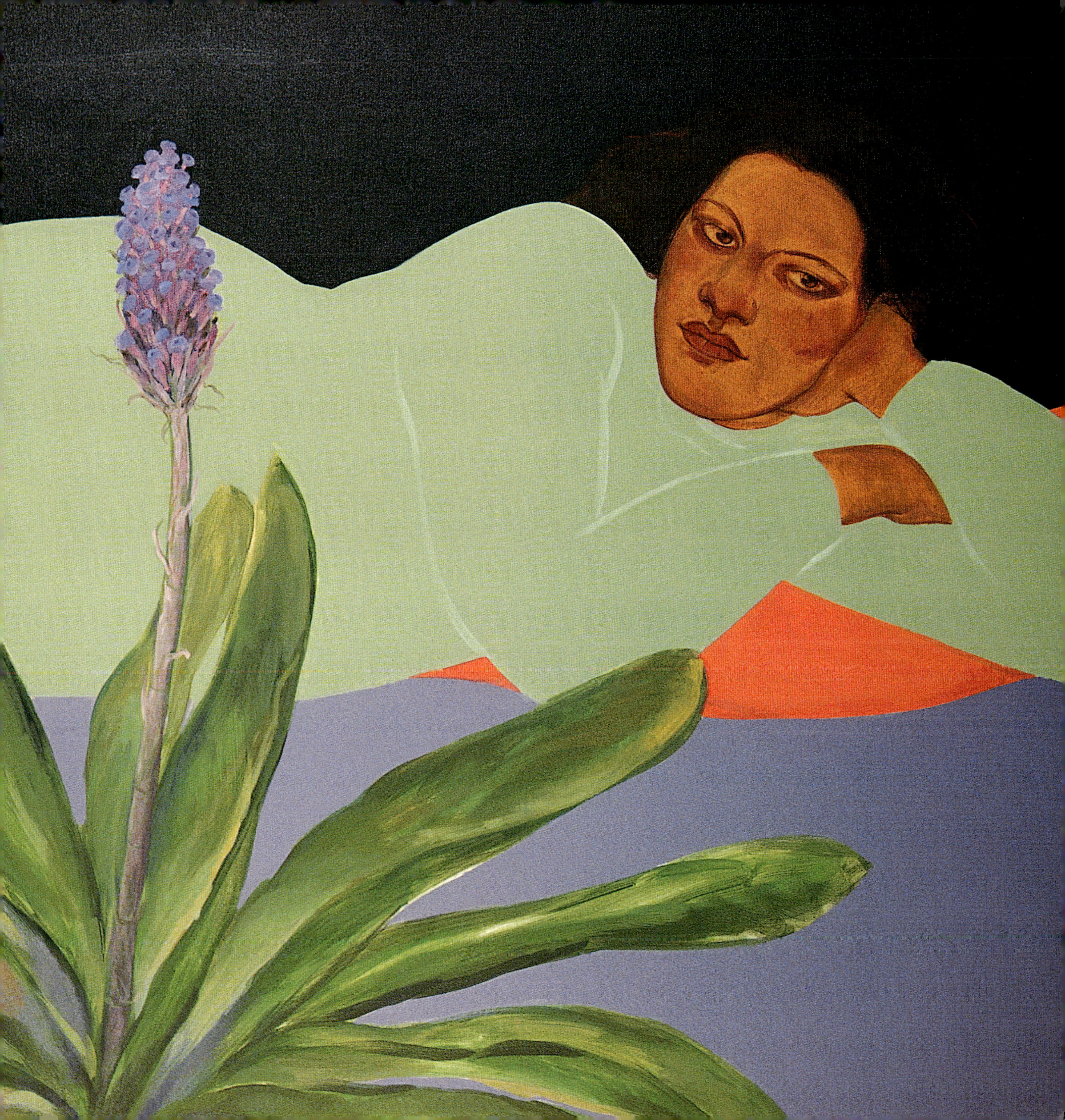

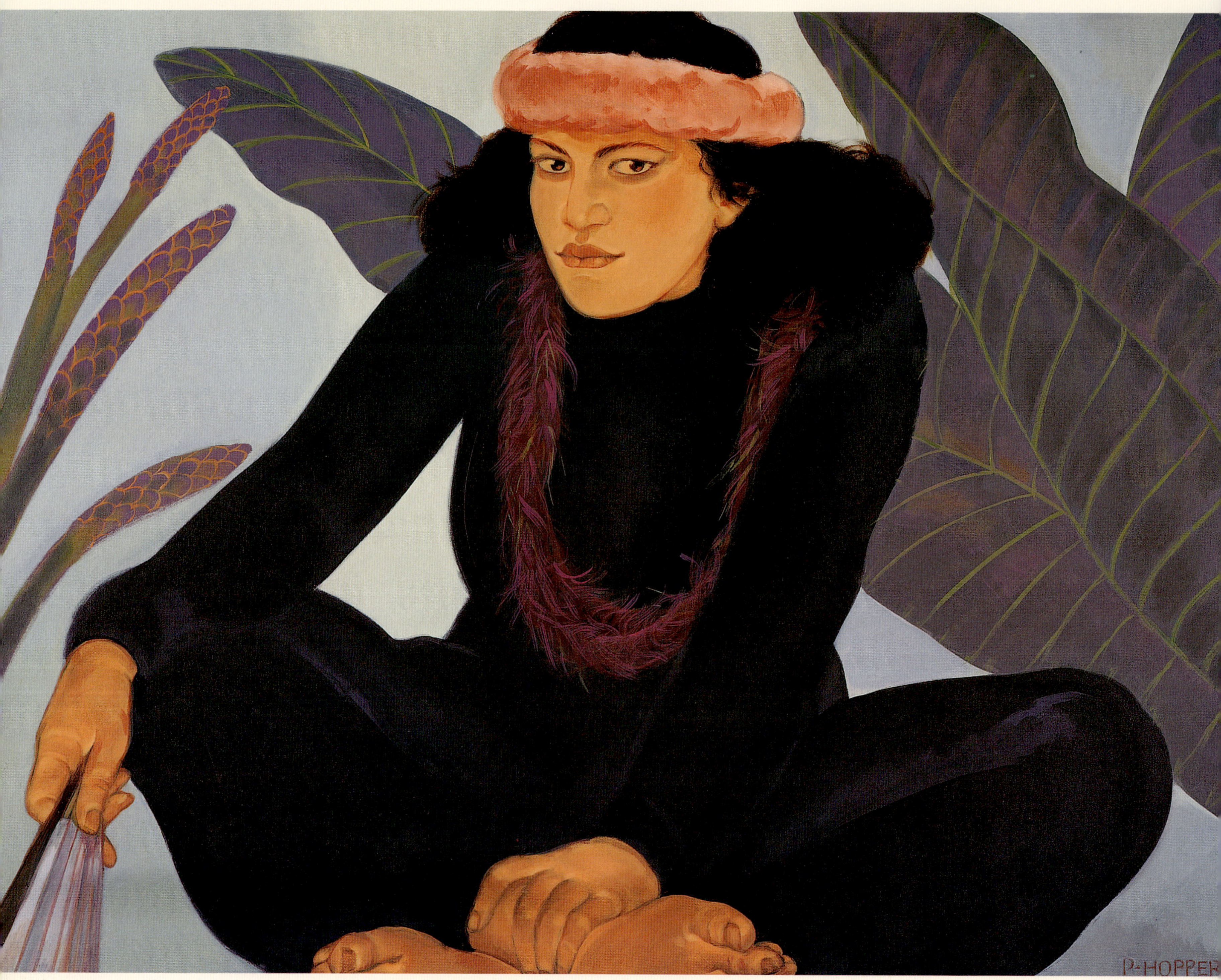
P-HOPPER

Feather Lei
4 x 5 feet, acrylic on canvas, circa 1995
Private collection

16

Okapaka

6 x 4 feet, acrylic on canvas, 1987

Private collection

{OPPOSITE} *Untitled*
4 x 5 feet, acrylic on canvas, 1993
Private collection

Untitled
4 x 6 feet, acrylic on canvas, 1991
Private collection

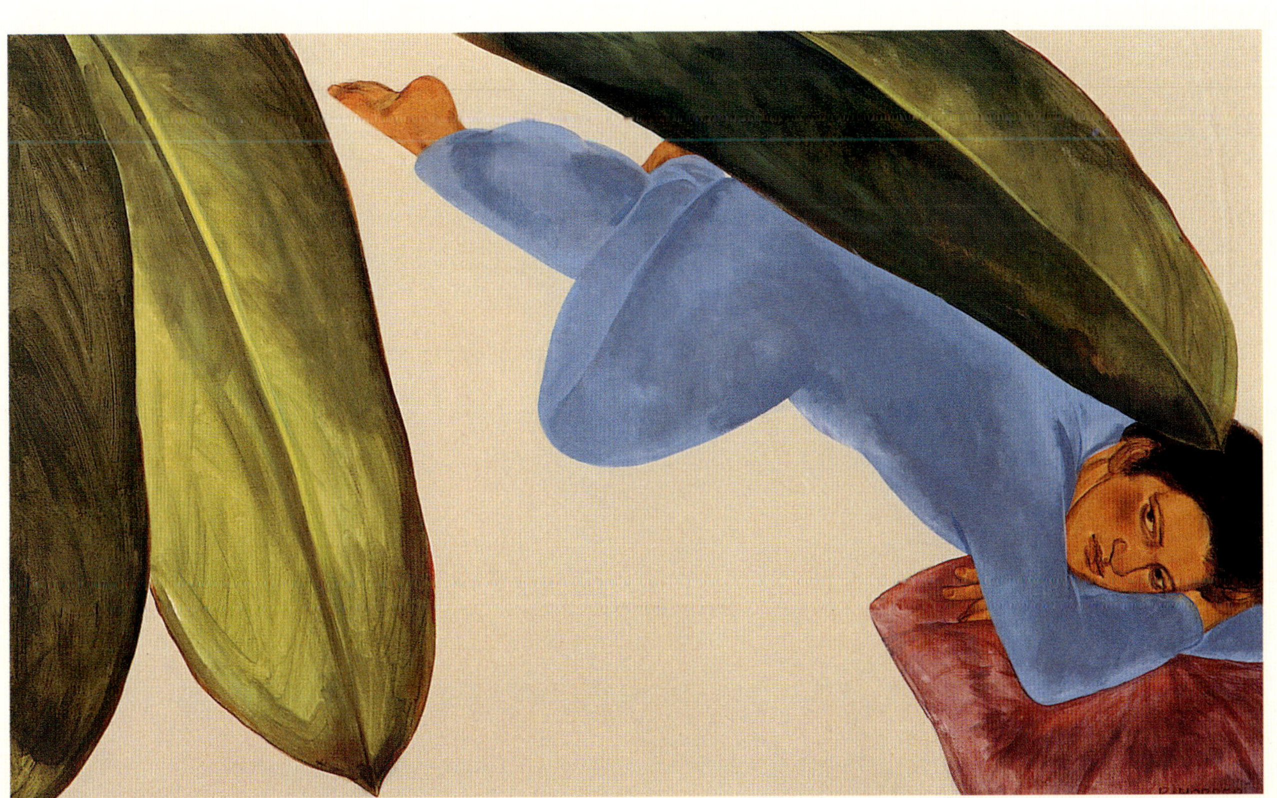

20

Mai`a
4 x 4 feet, acrylic on canvas, 1992
Private collection

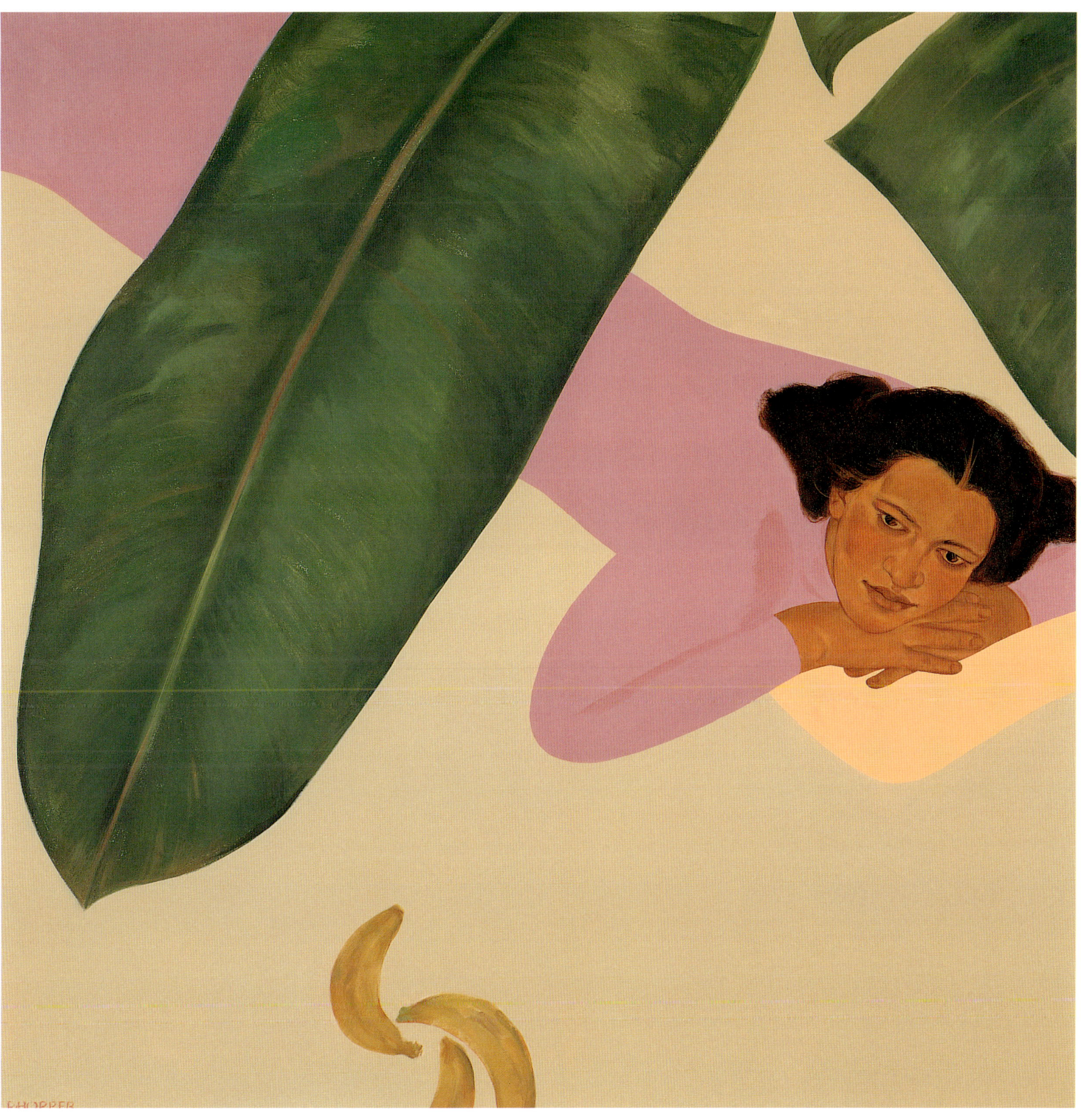

LEAVES

Leaves, especially banana leaves, have been an important element in my work. They grow outside of my studio and look particularly lush and beautiful around 4PM, when the sunlight filters through them.

Untitled
4 x 4 feet, acrylic on canvas, 1992
Private collection

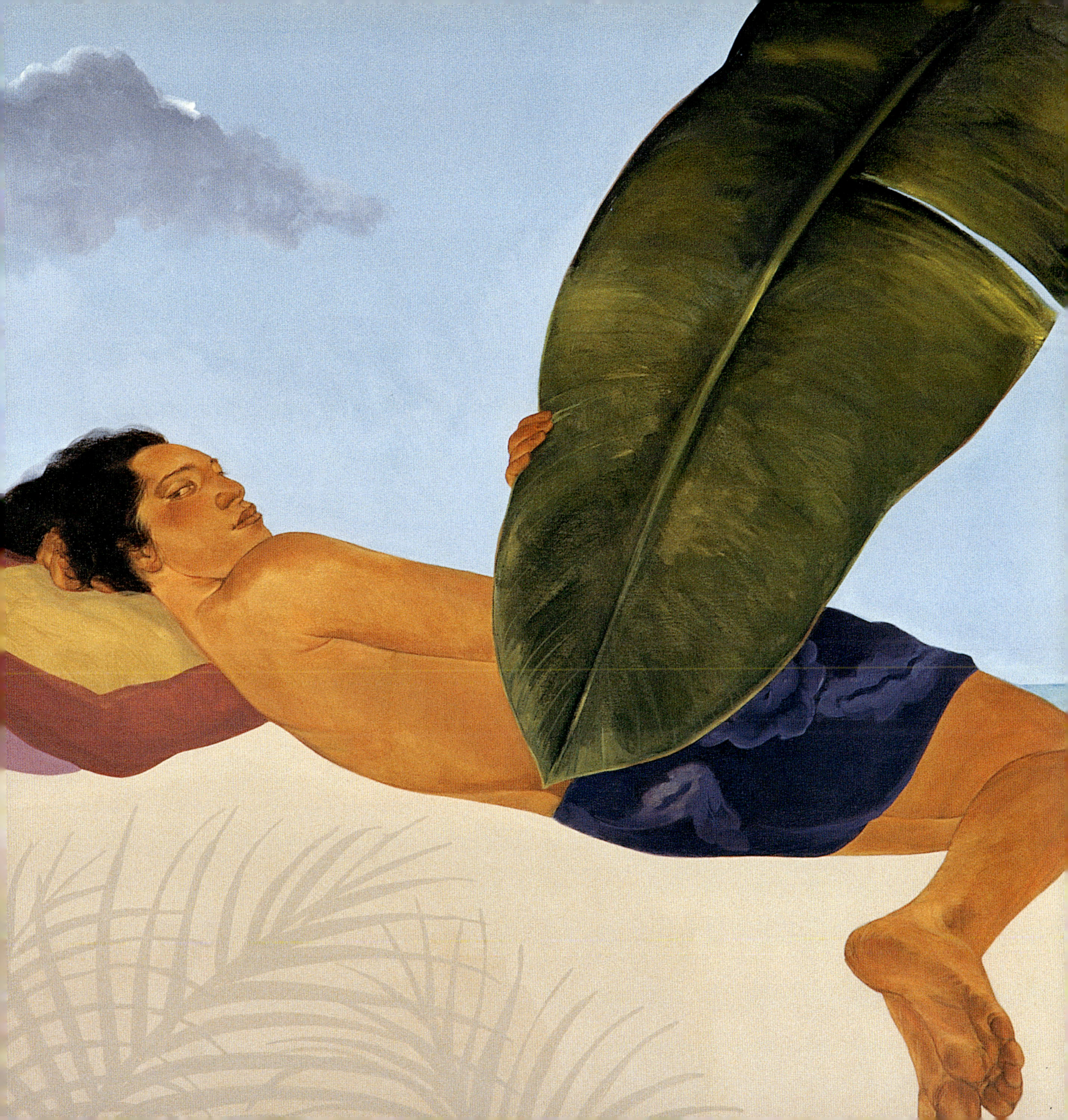

BANANAS

In Hawaiian, *mai`a* means "banana." This painting was inspired by the ornamental bananas that grow in my yard.

Pola (banana blossom)
3 x 2 feet, acrylic on canvas, 1999
Collection of the artist

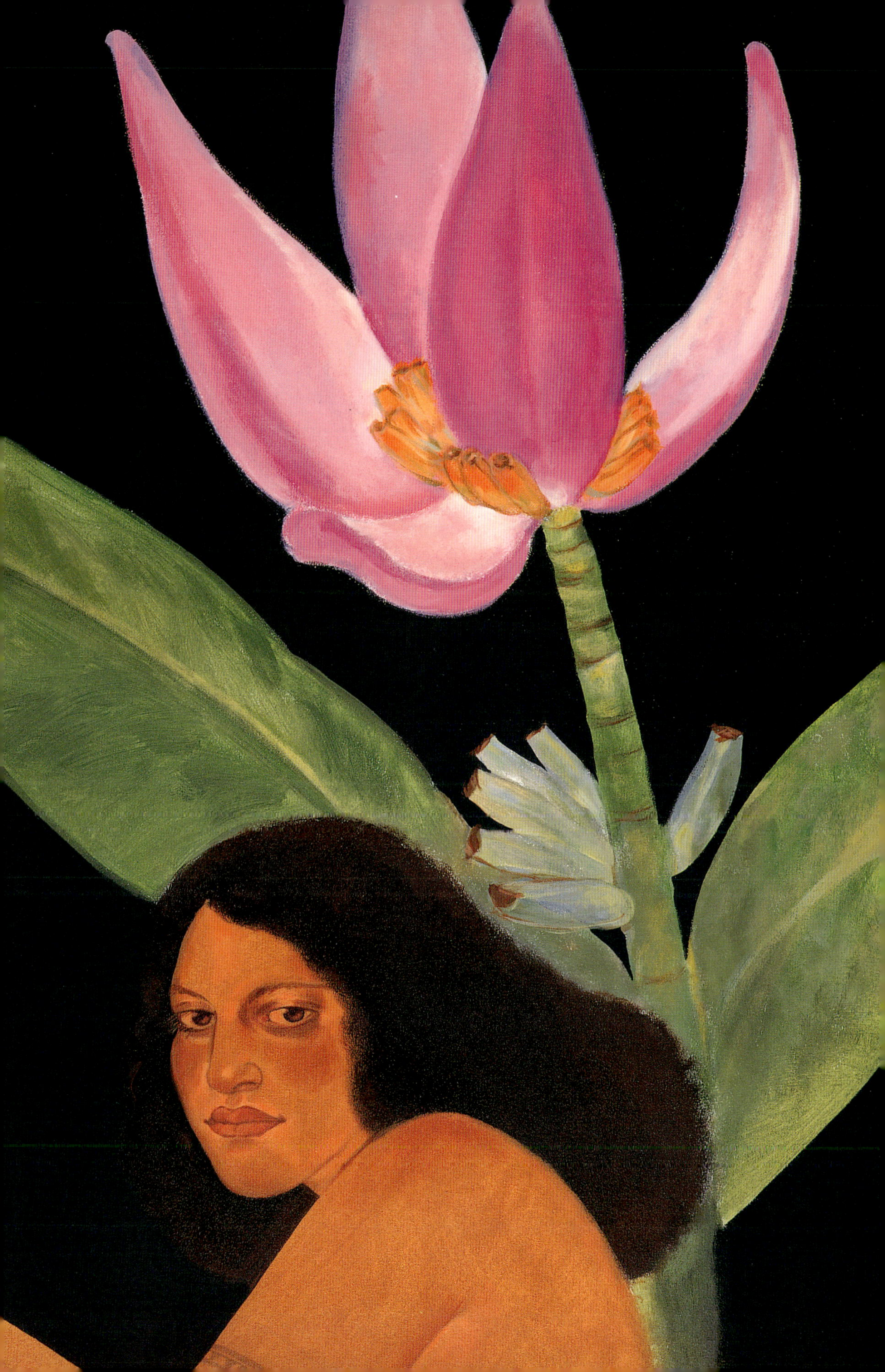

HELECONIA

Heleconia also grows in great profusion, by the stream running below my studio.

Heleconia
3 x 2 feet, acrylic on canvas, 1999
Private collection

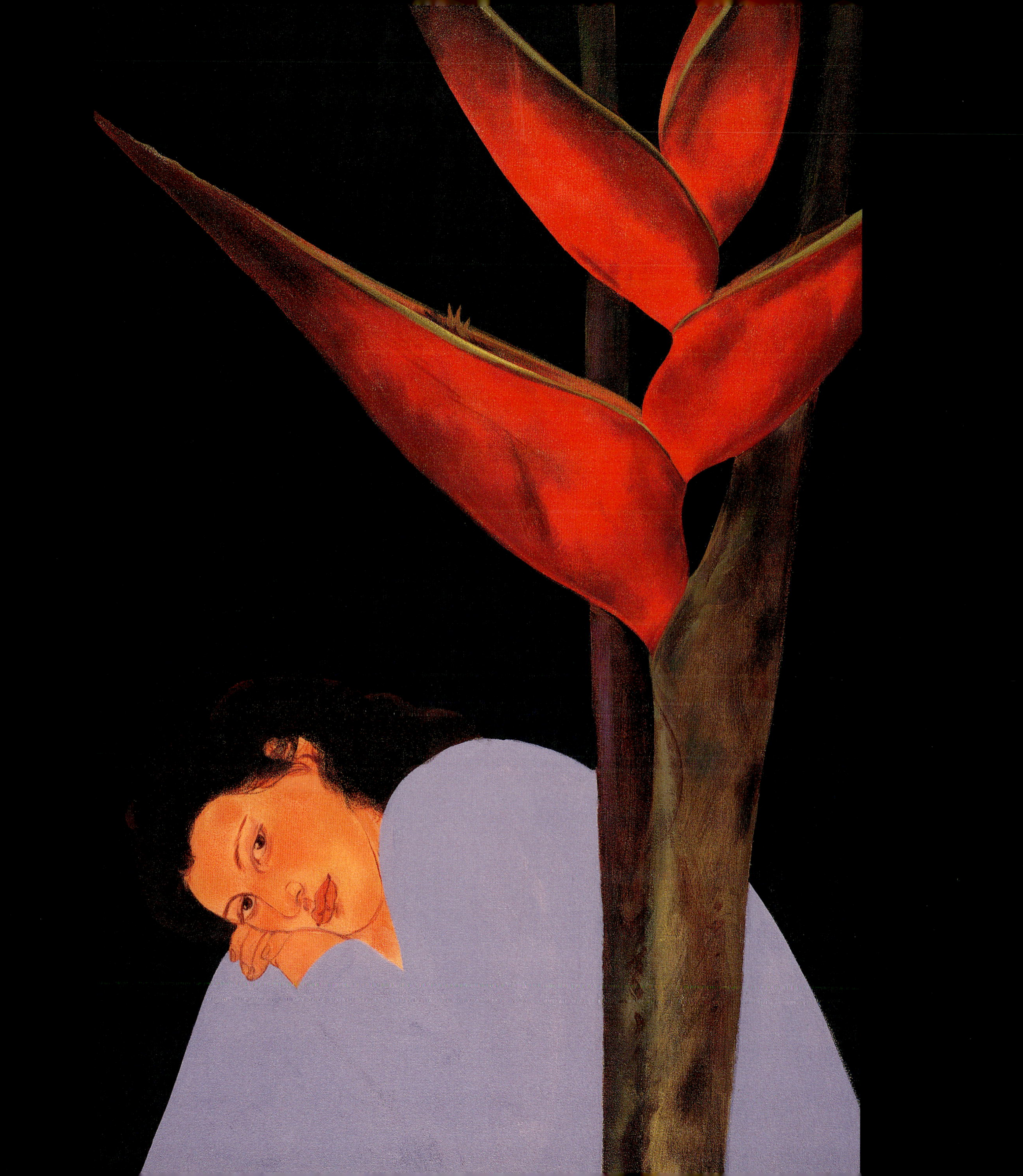

Akala Wahine (pink lady)
2 x 3 feet, acrylic on canvas, 2000
Collection of the artist

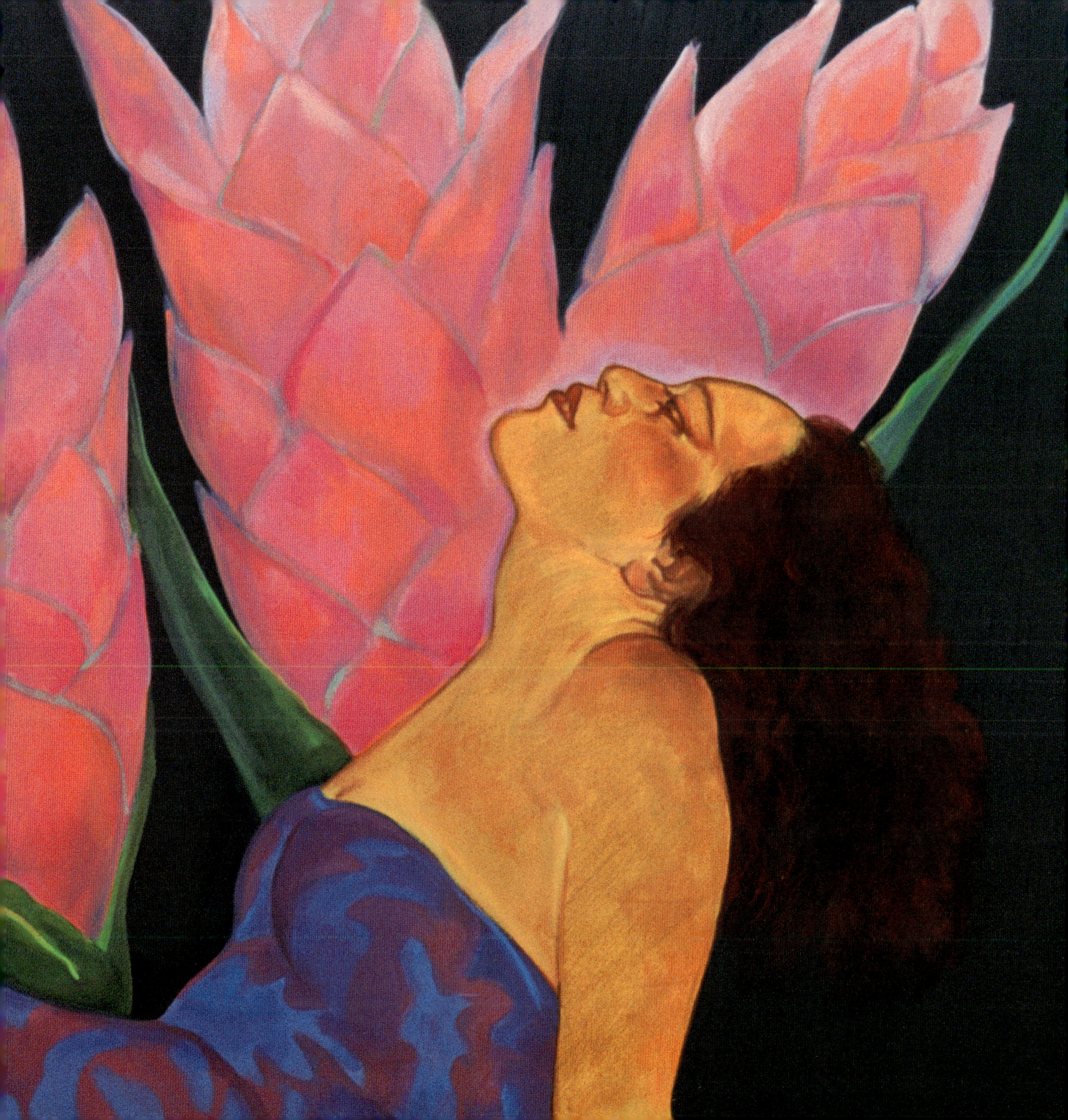

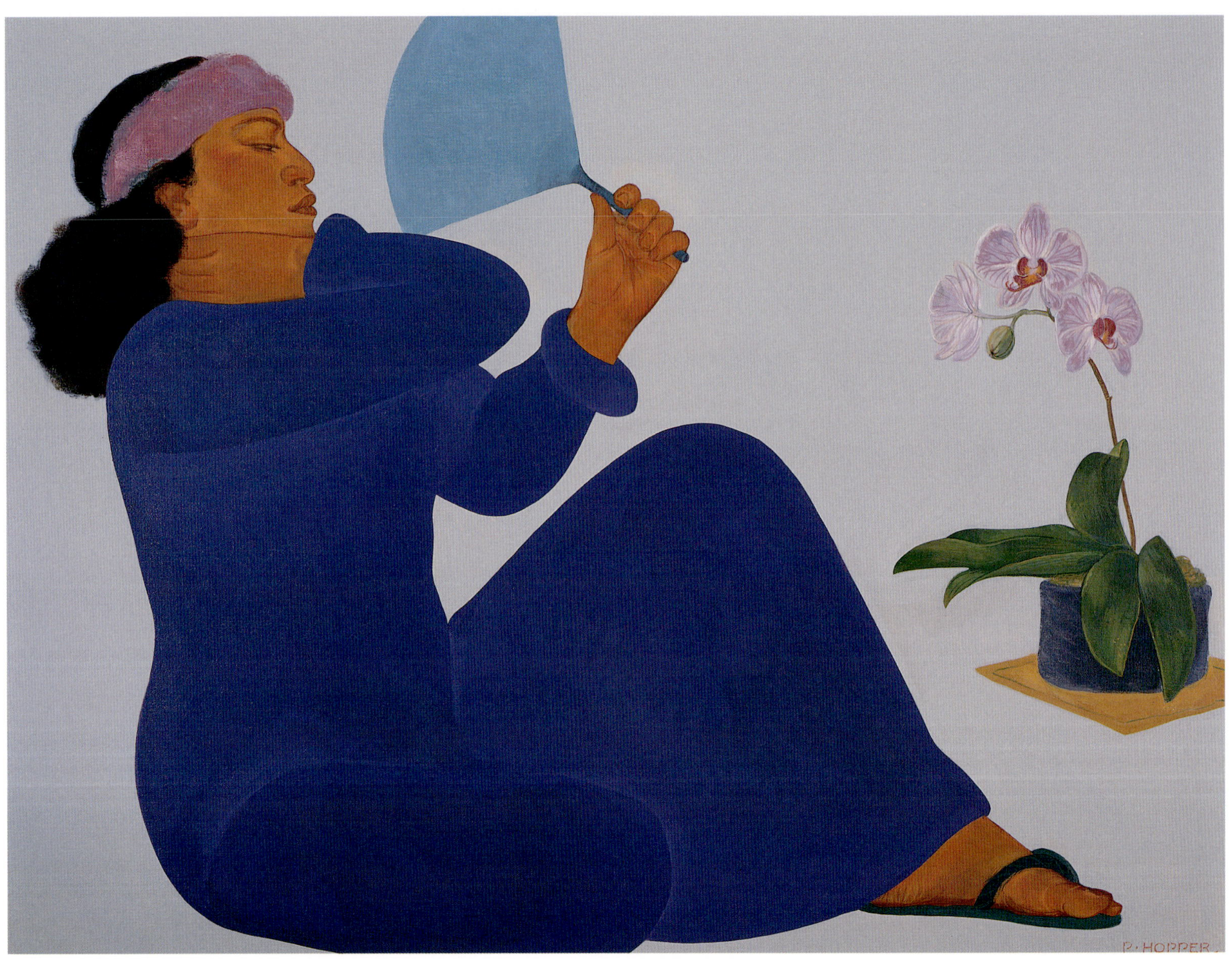
P. HOPPER.

Blue Fan
4 x 5 feet, acrylic on canvas, 1985
Private collection

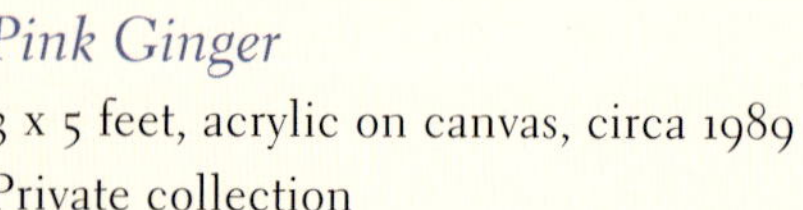

Pink Ginger

32 3 x 5 feet, acrylic on canvas, circa 1989

Private collection

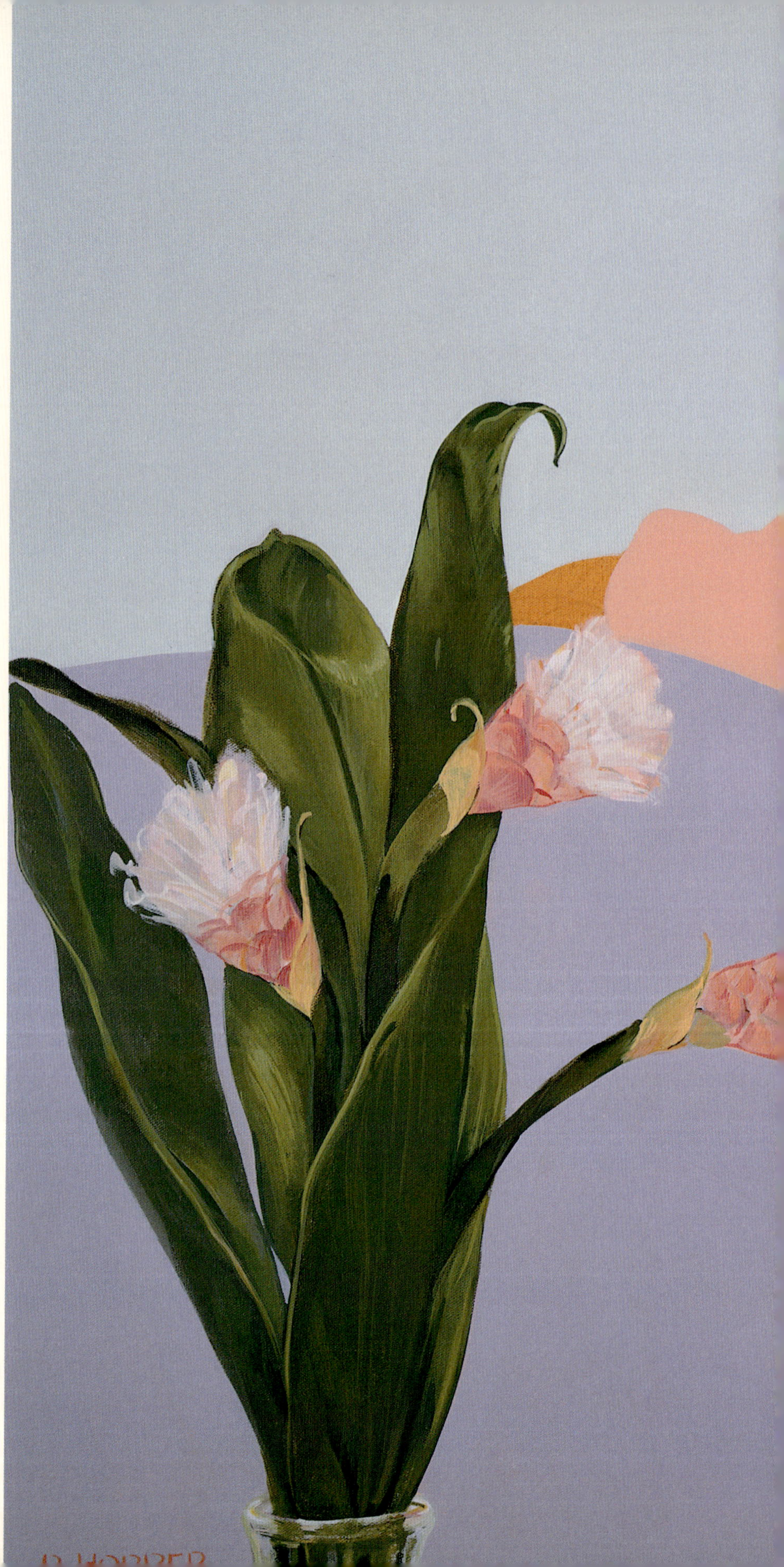

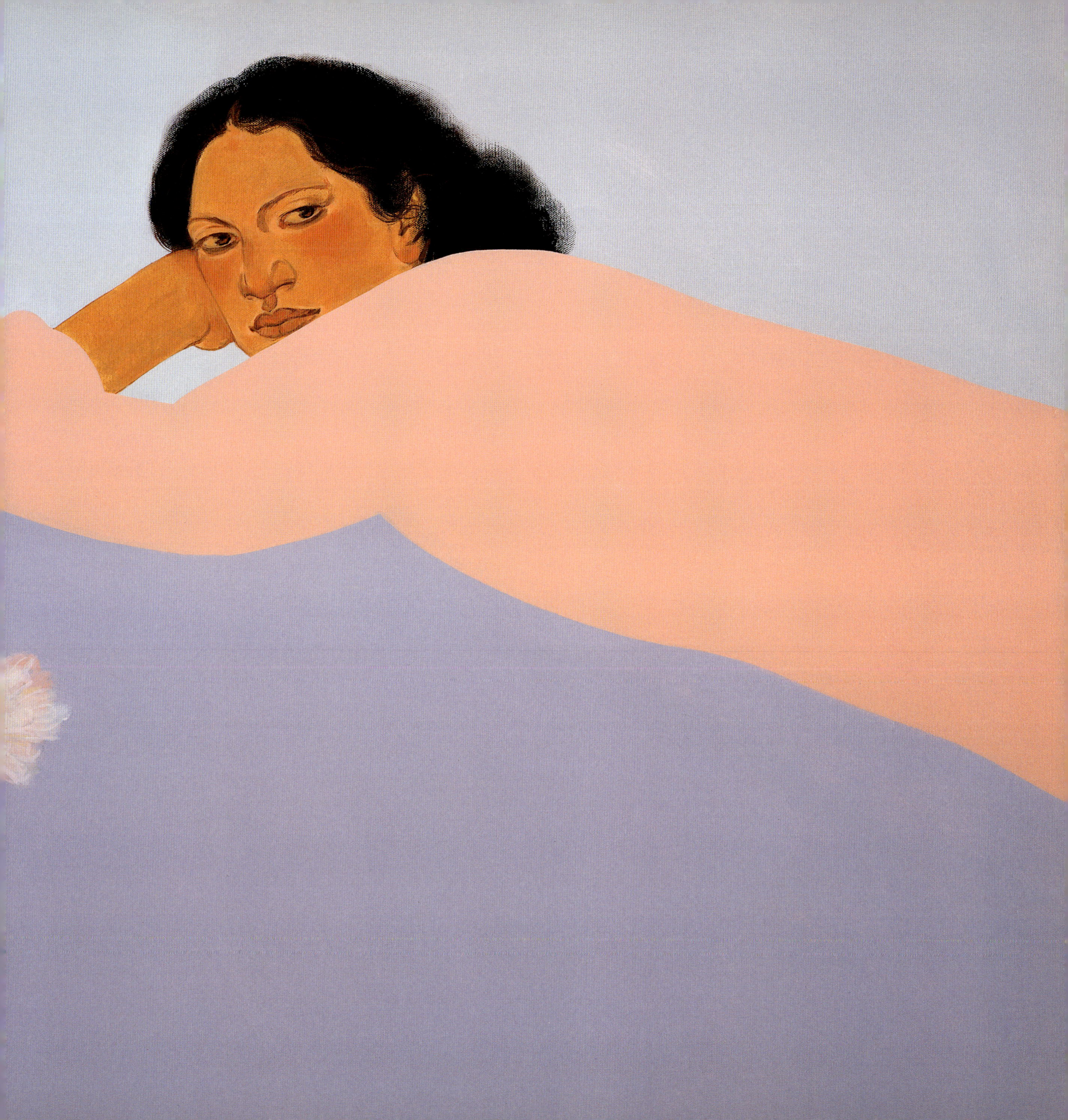

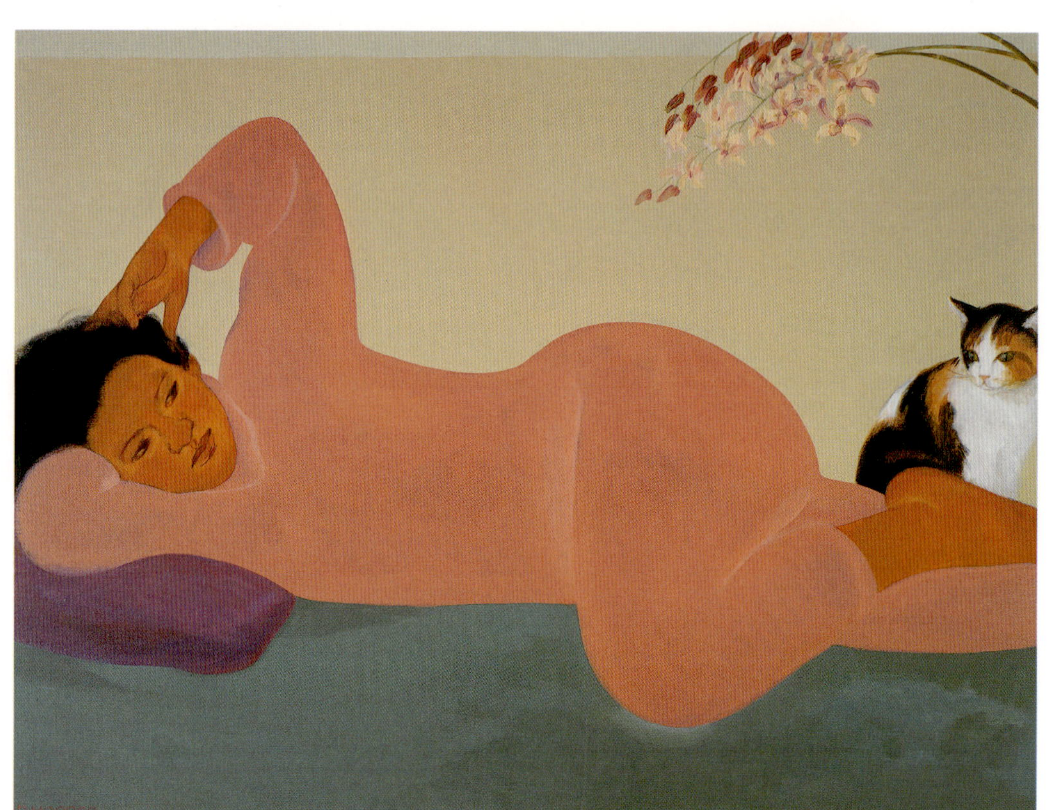

Calico Popoki
2 x 3 feet, acrylic on canvas, 1987
Private collection

{OPPOSITE} *Black Popoki*
4 x 5 feet, acrylic on canvas, 1986
Private collection

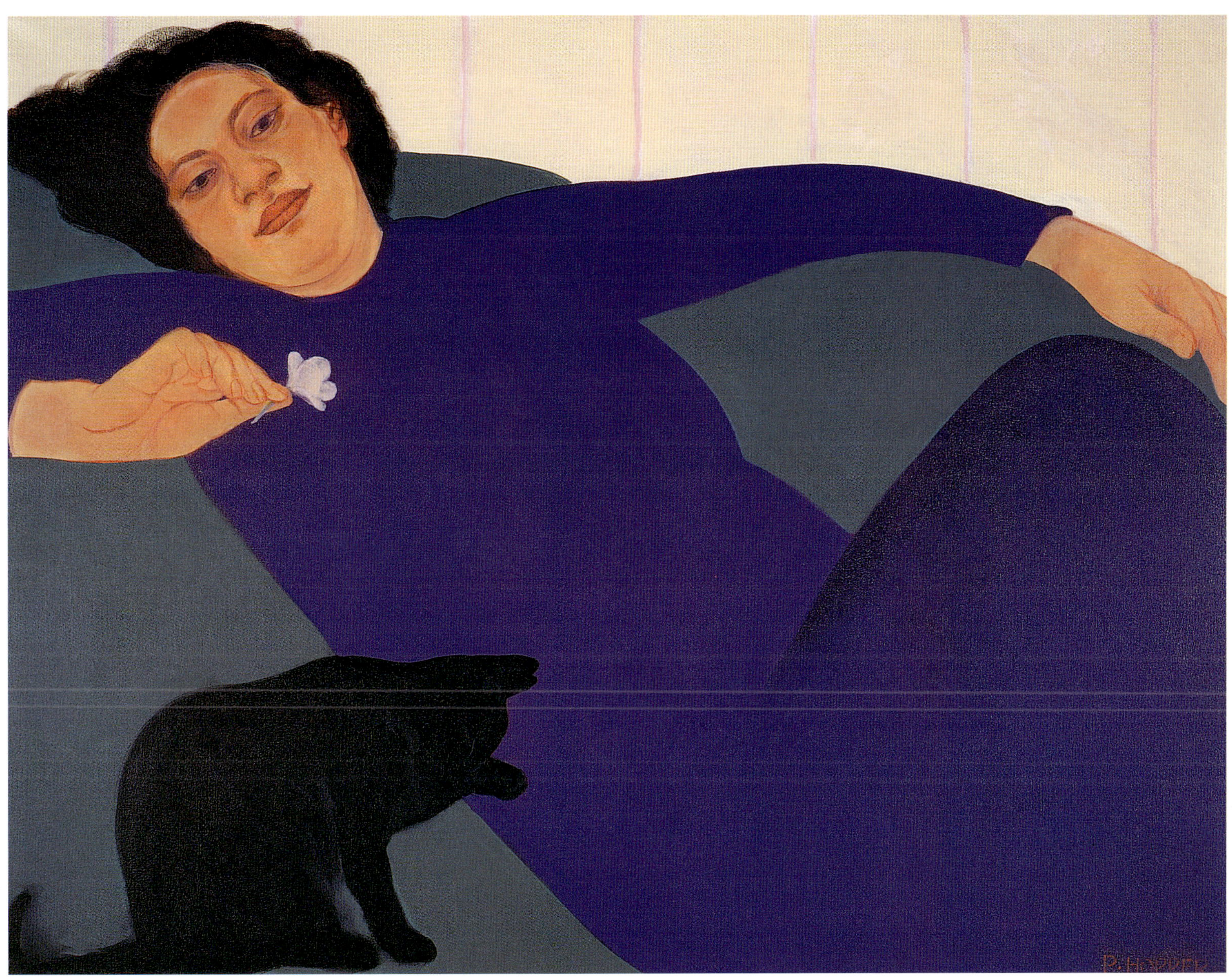

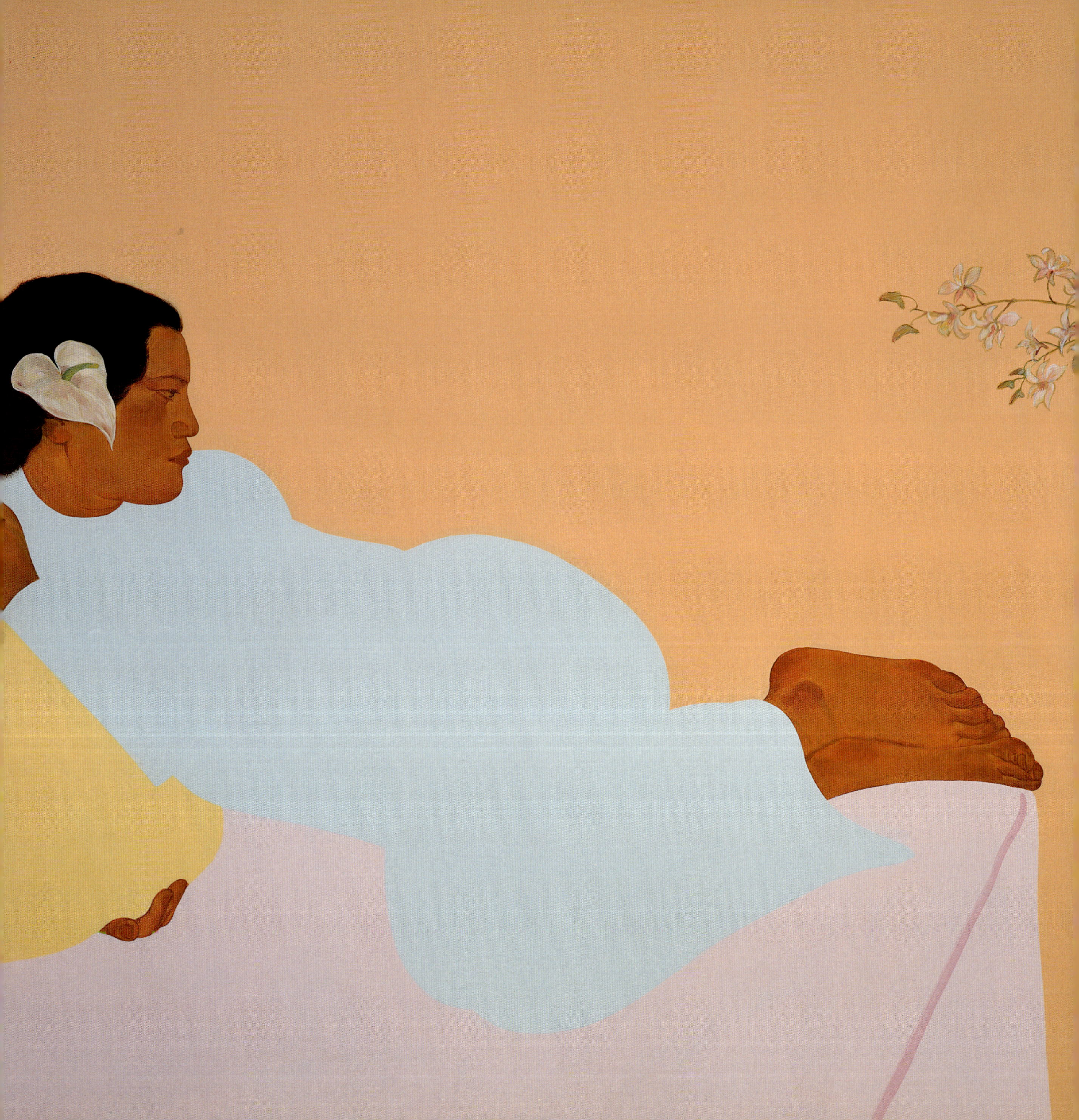

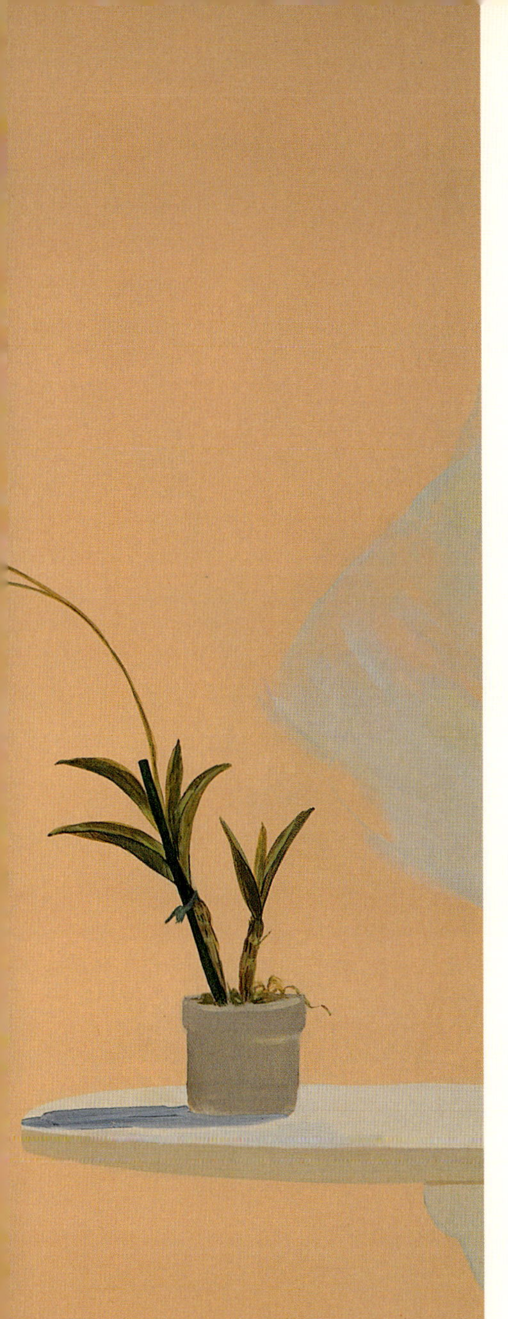

Kakahiaka (morning)
4 x 5 feet, acrylic on canvas, 1985
Private collection

Green Curtain

38 2 x 3 feet, acrylic on canvas, 1997

Private collection

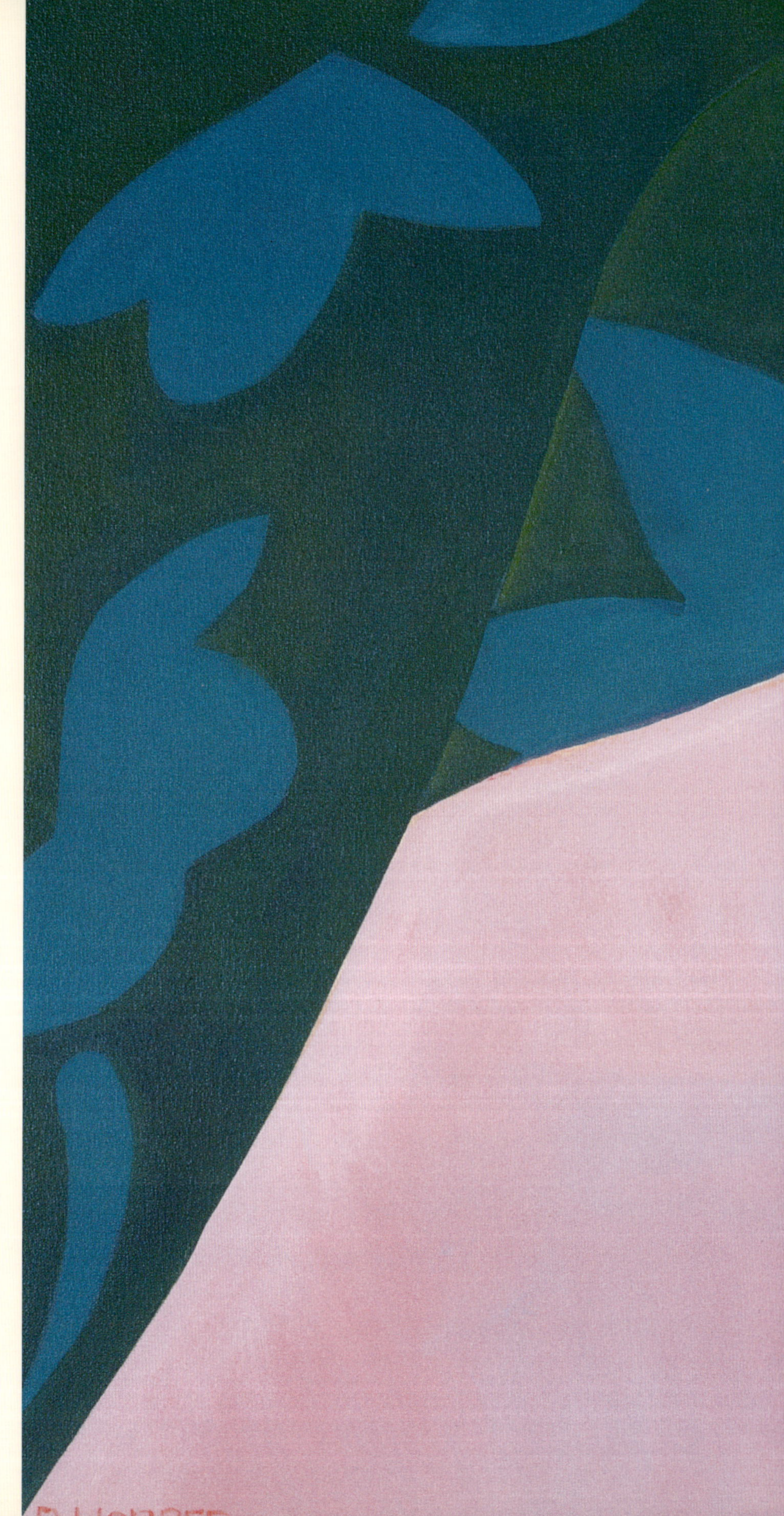

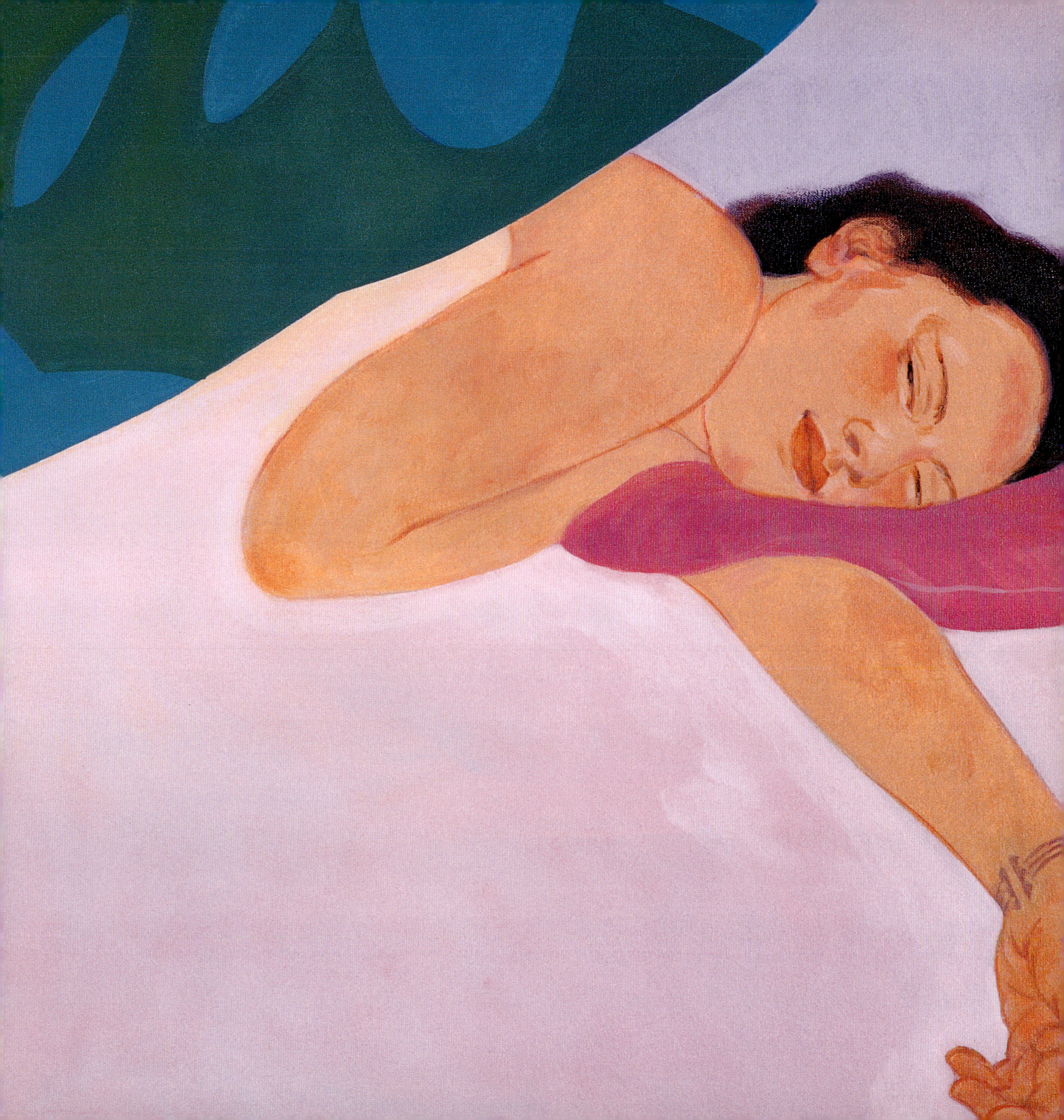

PORTRAIT

I'm reluctant to accept portrait commissions, but a beautiful Asian woman convinced me to do hers. She even provided a picture of the antique kimono she wanted to be wearing. The finished painting didn't please her, so I changed the face, opened the front of the kimono, and sold it in my gallery.

Madame Butterfly
4 x 6 feet, acrylic on canvas, 1988
Private collection

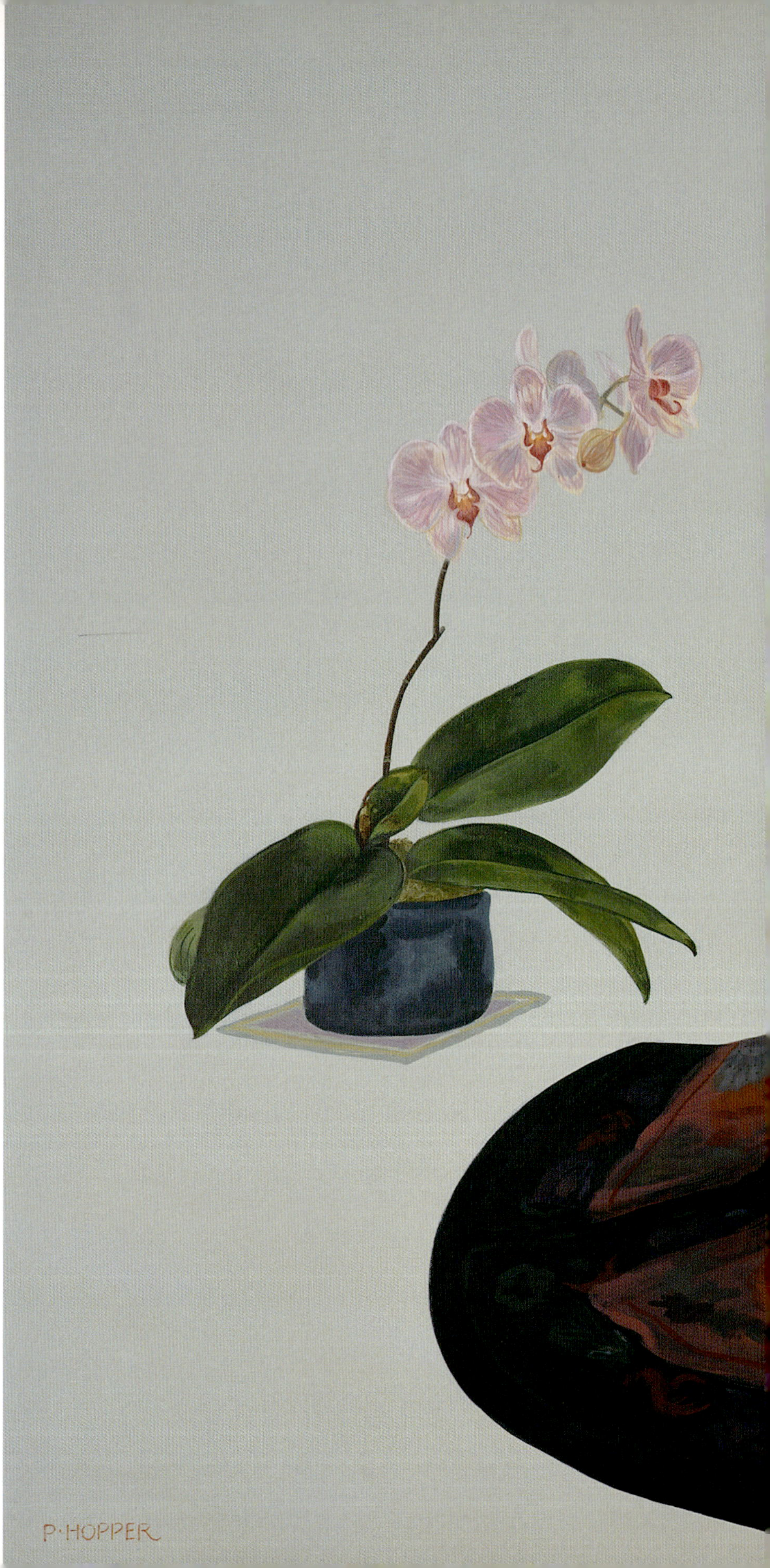

P·HOPPER

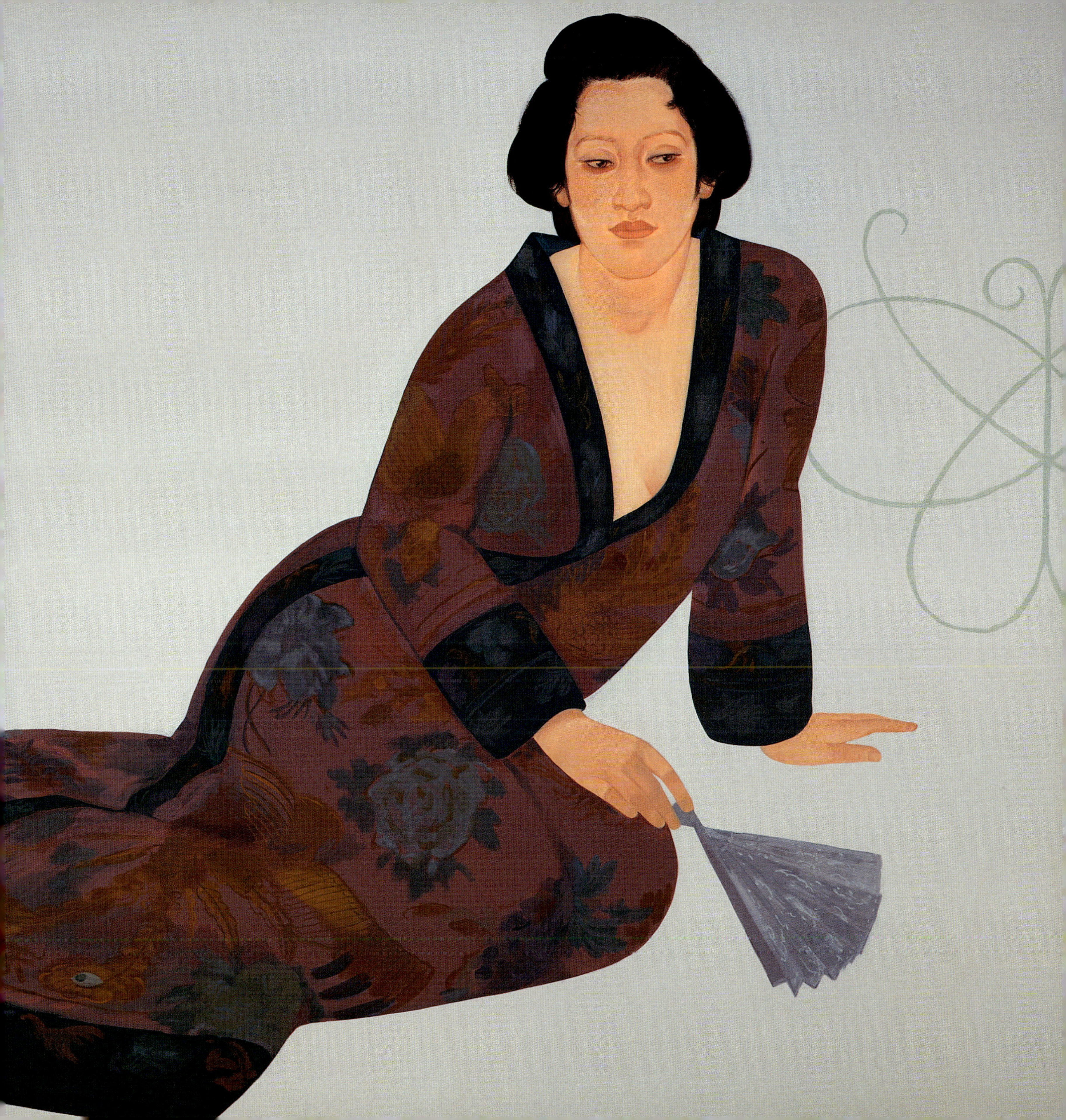

MOTORCYCLES

A shiny, well-loved bike is a beautiful object. All the working parts are exposed and, to me, mysterious. I love the chrome shapes—so full of potential energy. A motorcycle is a symbol of independence, freedom, and adventure. To be sitting on all that power is like riding the wind. If I were twenty years younger, I'd have one.

1947 Knucklehead
4 x 8 feet, acrylic and pastel on board, 1996
Private collection

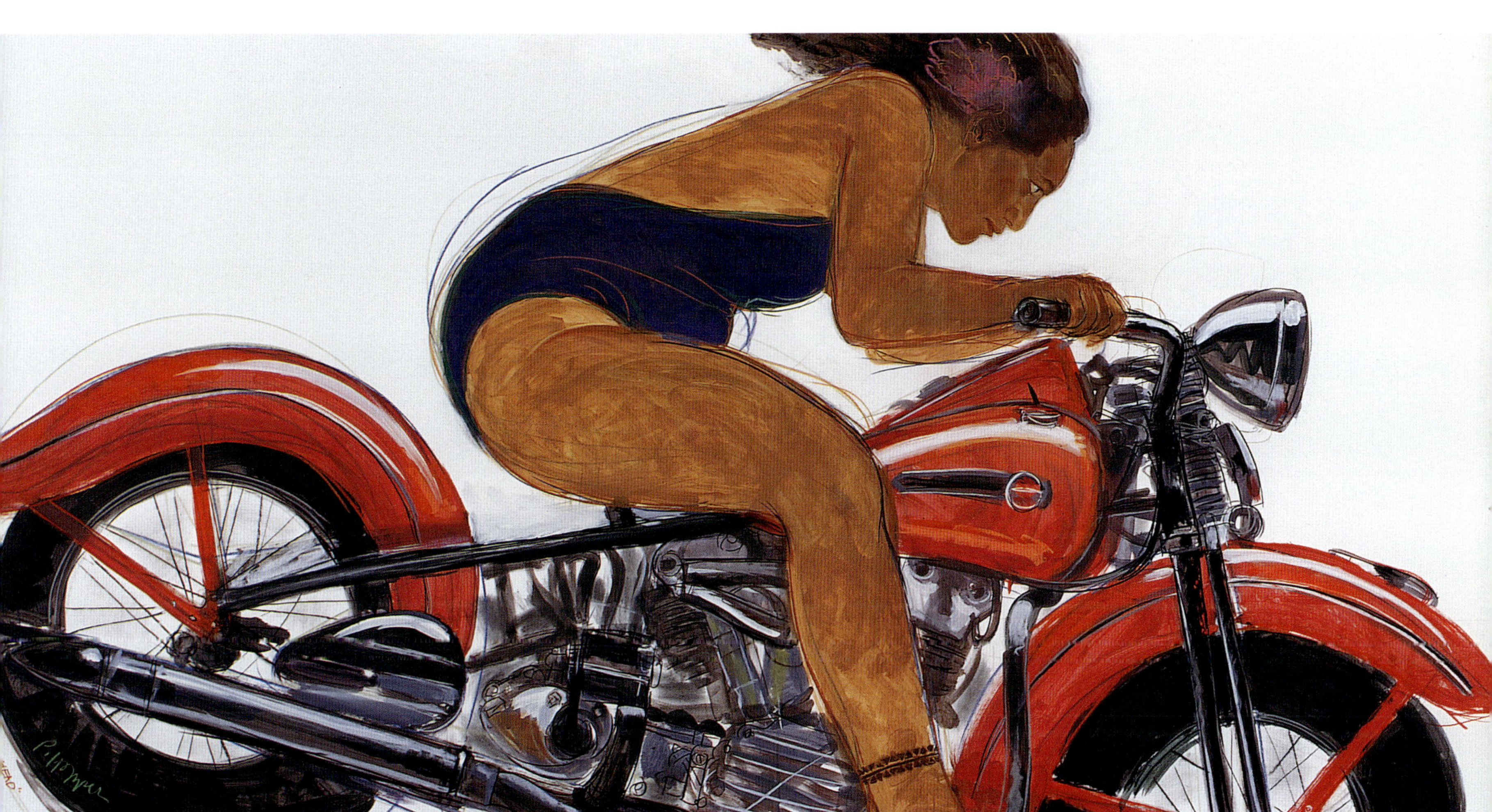

Harley Series
4 x 8 feet, acrylic and pastel on board, 1996
Private collection

{OPPOSITE} *Harley Series*
4 x 8 feet, acrylic and pastel on board, 1996
Private collection

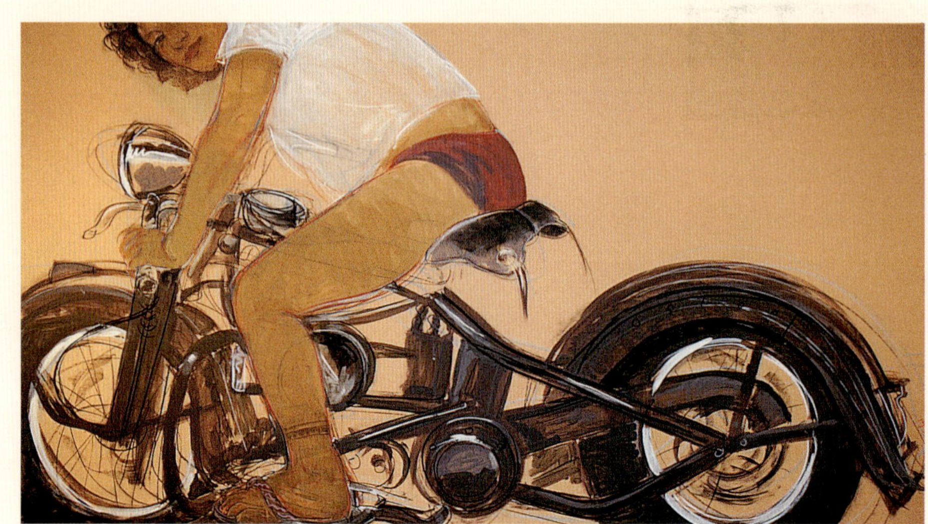

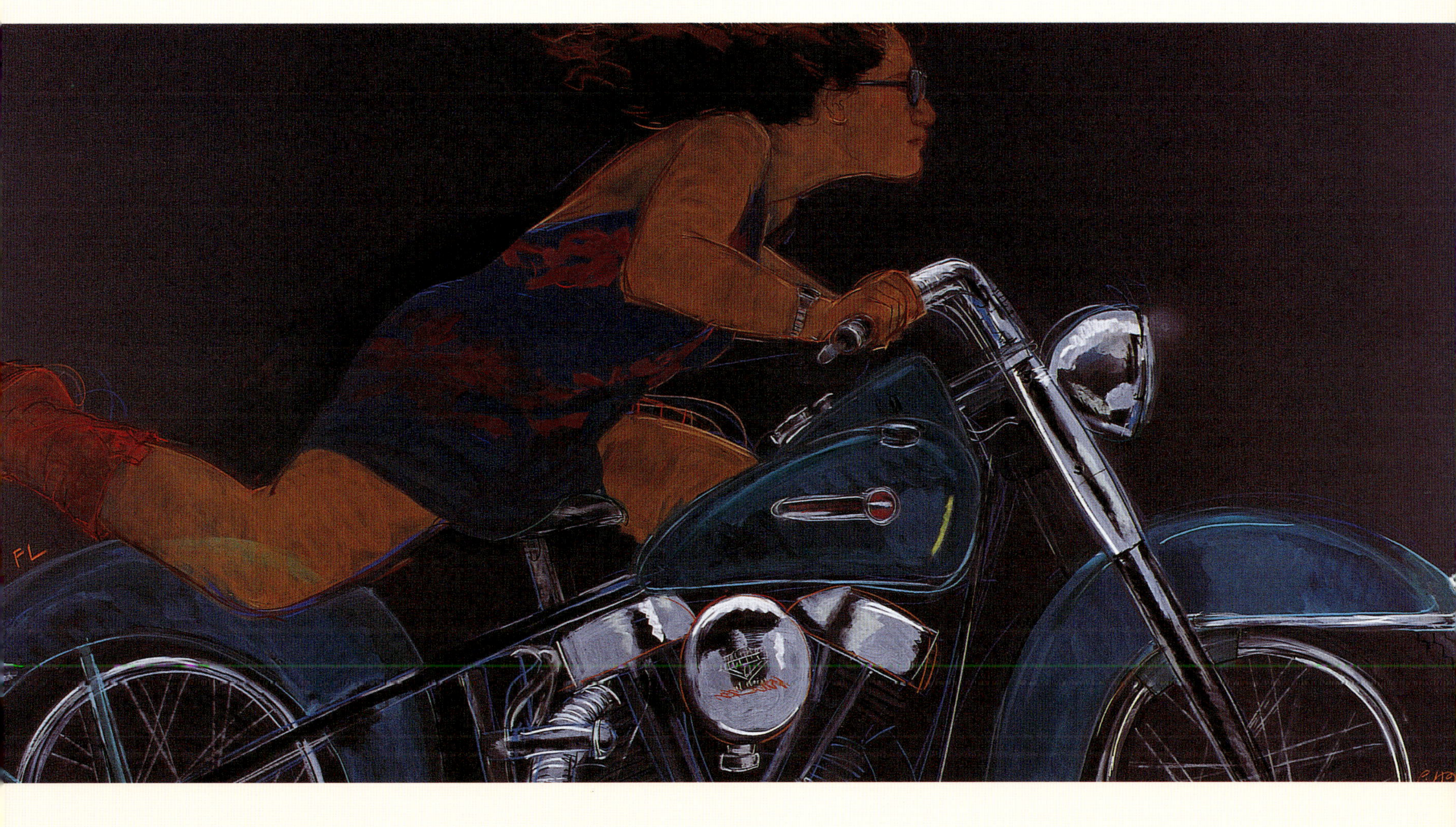

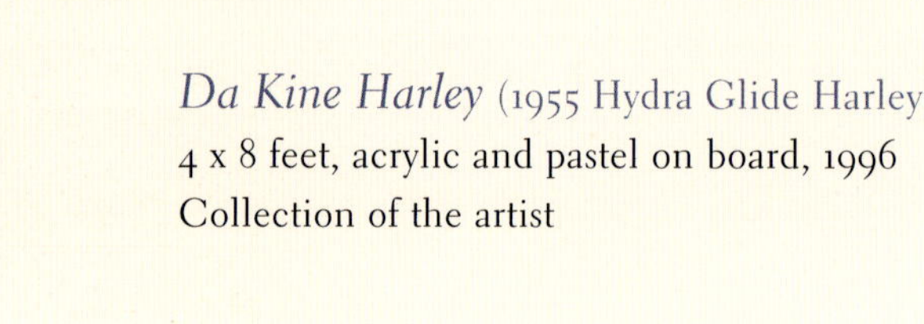

Da Kine Harley (1955 Hydra Glide Harley)
4 x 8 feet, acrylic and pastel on board, 1996
Collection of the artist

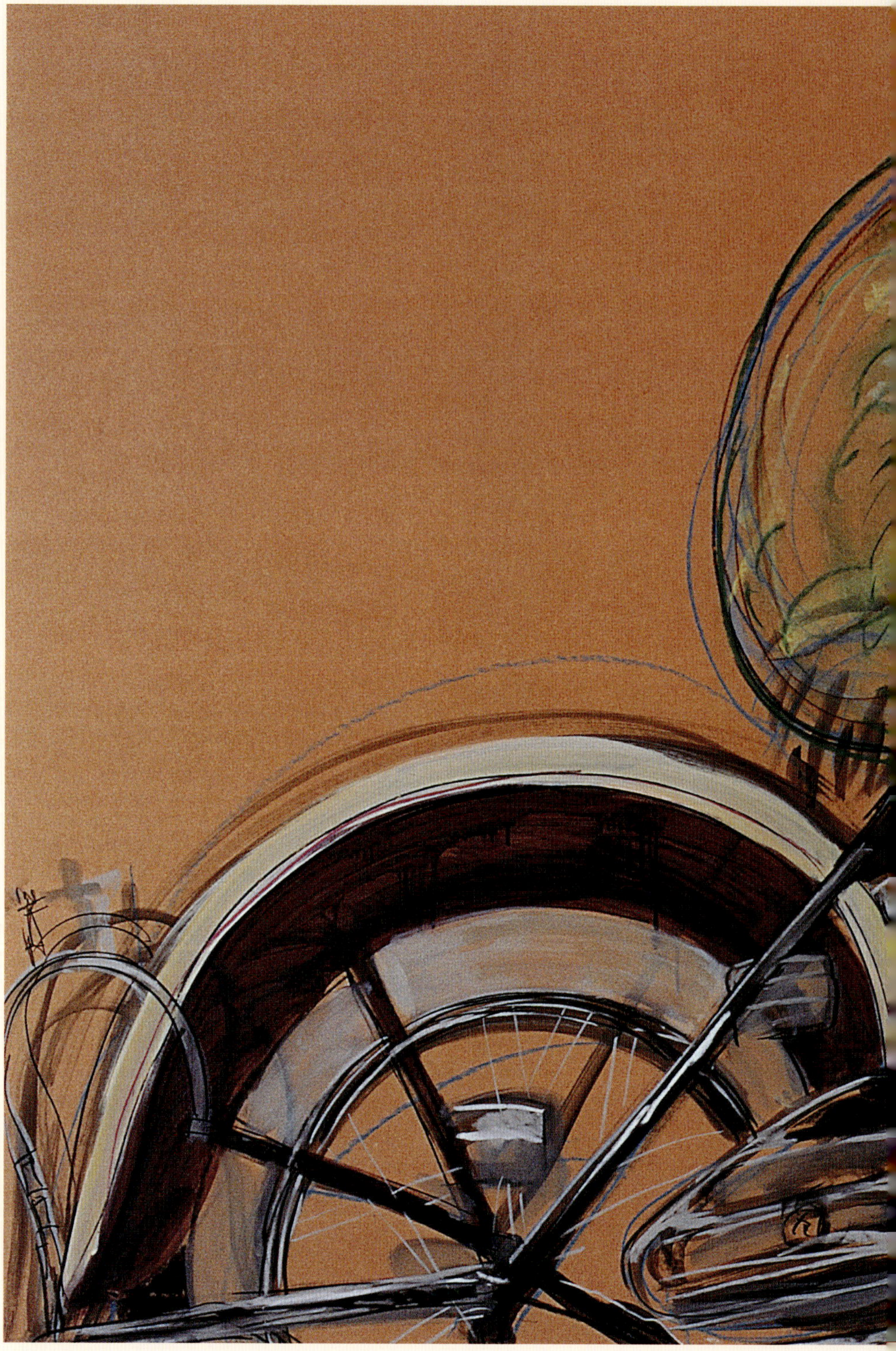

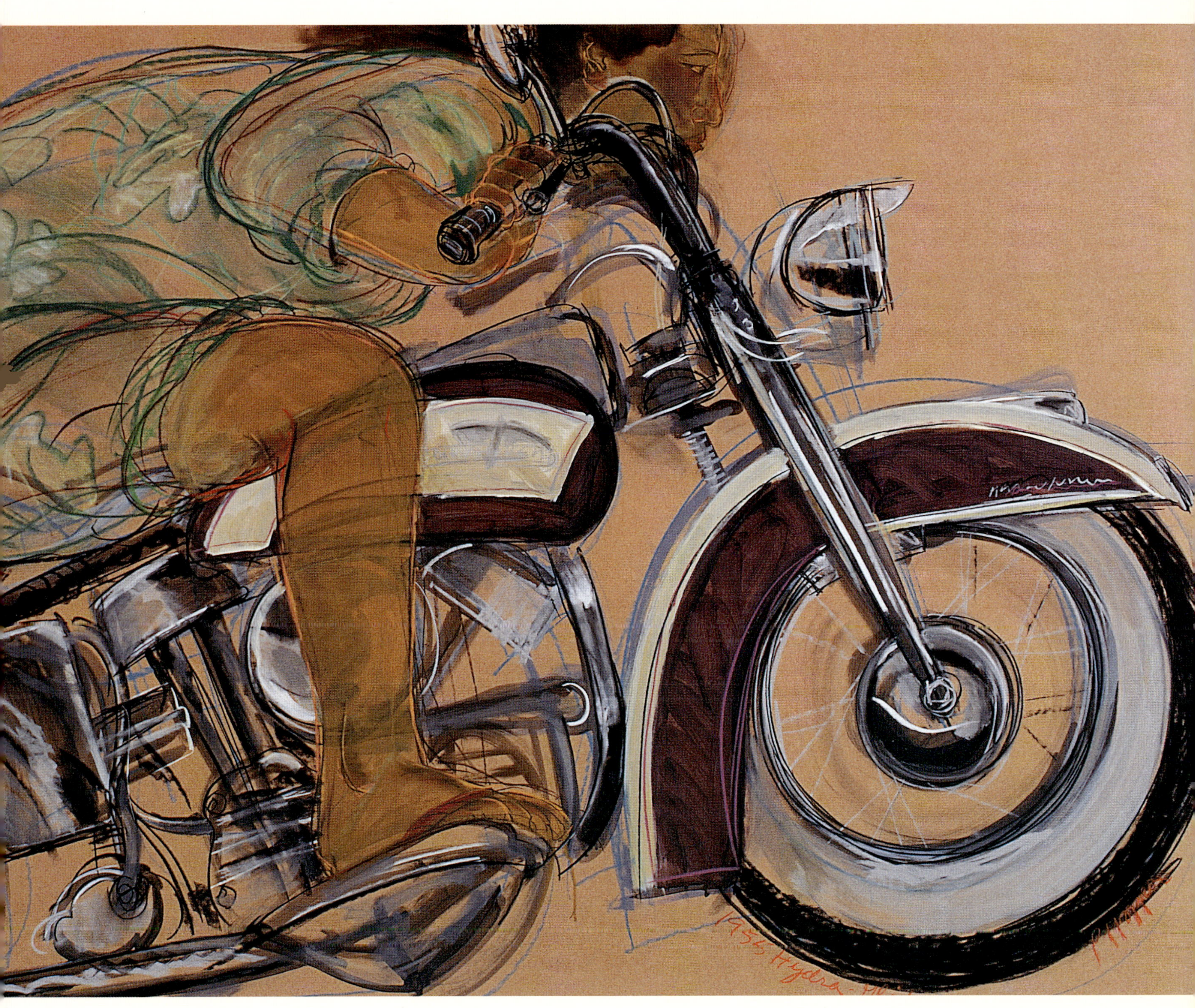

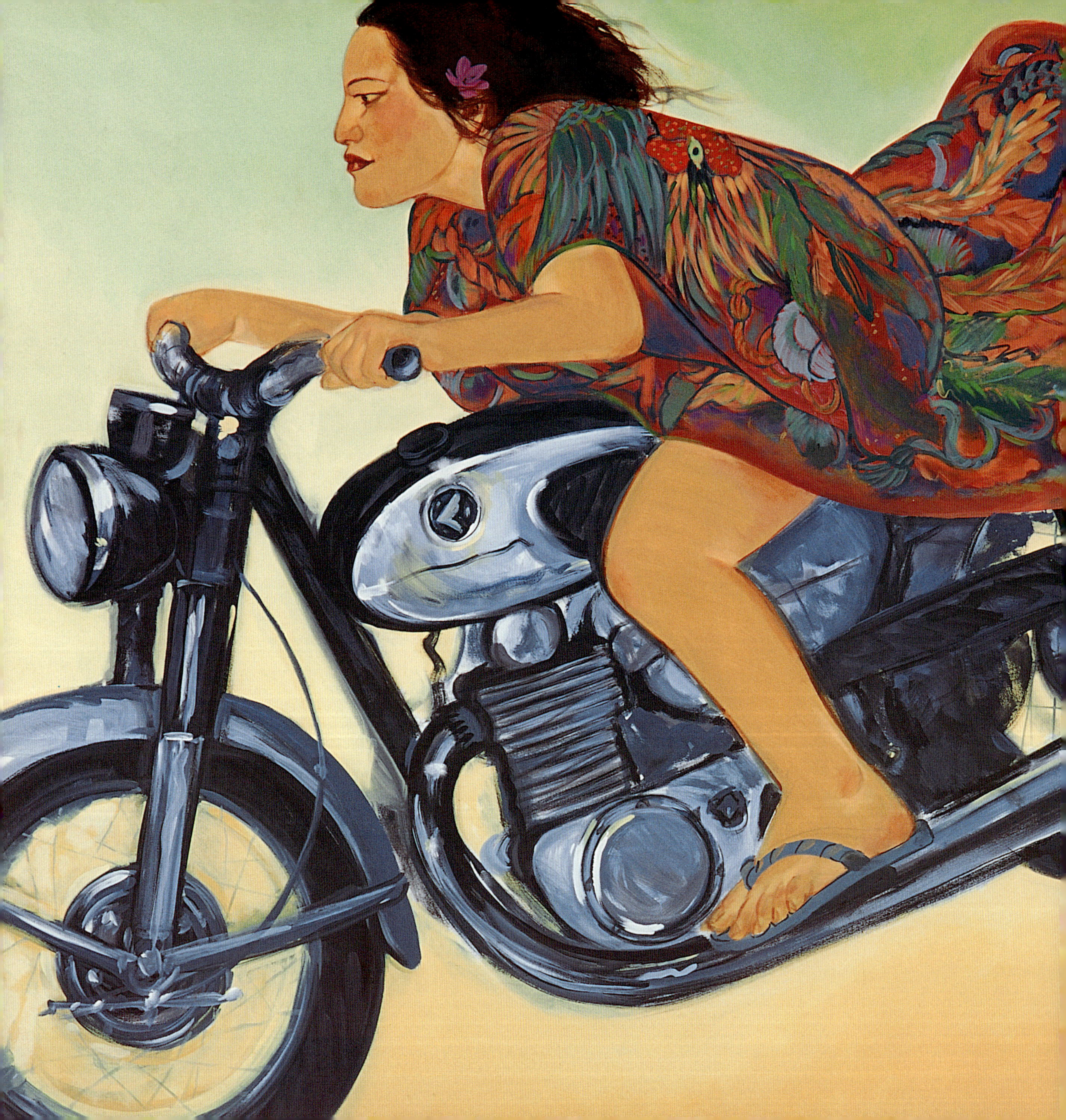

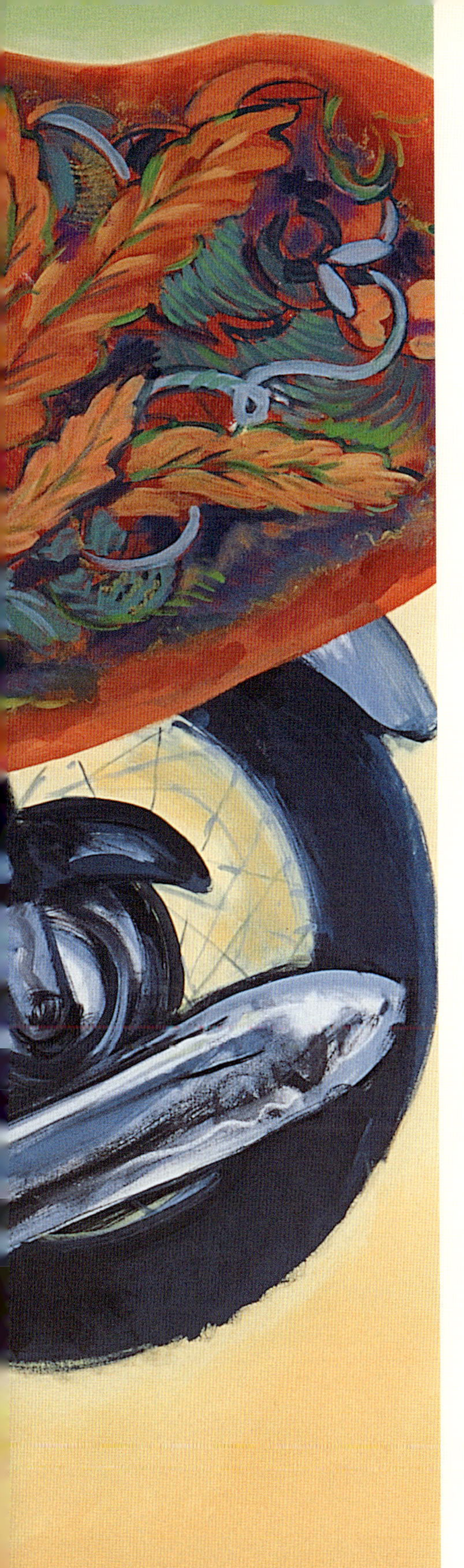

{OPPOSITE} *Flying Tita* (on a Suzuki)
4 x 5 feet, acrylic on canvas, 1999
Pegge Hopper Gallery, Honolulu

1958 DuoGlide
4 x 8 feet, acrylic and pastel on board, 1997
Private collection

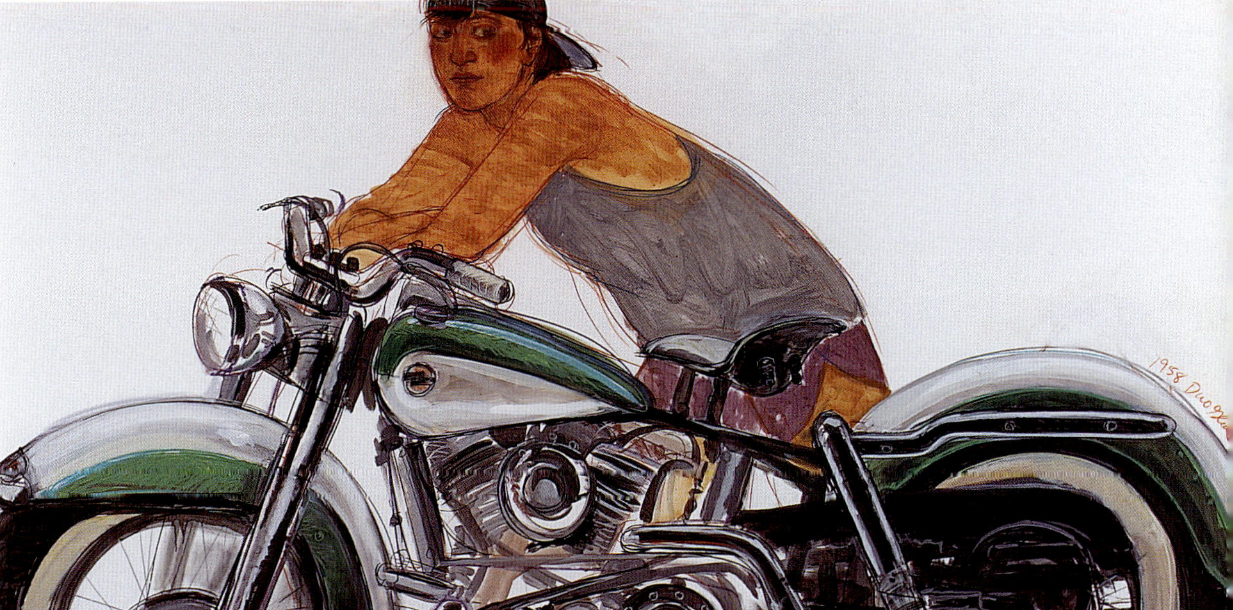

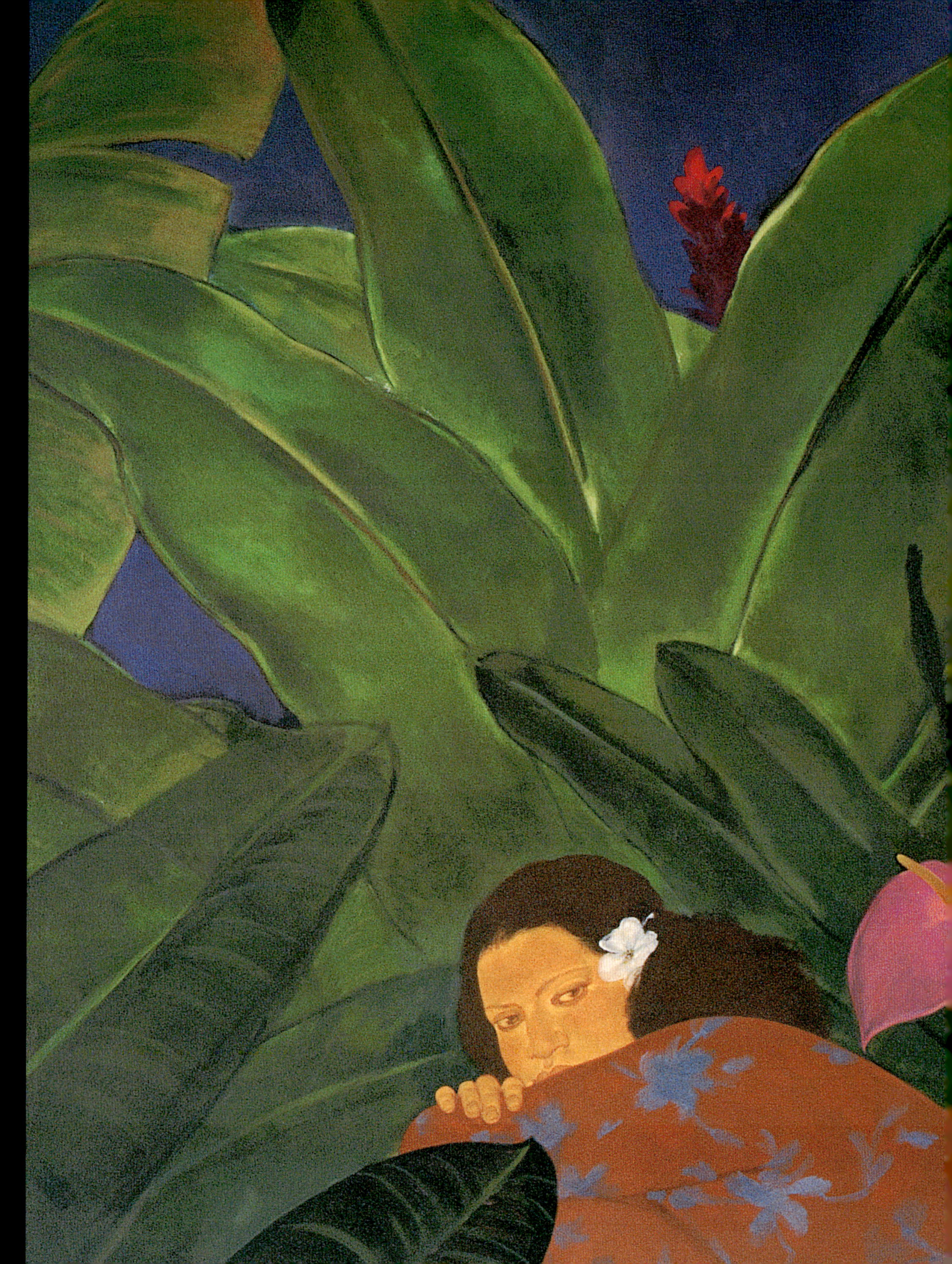

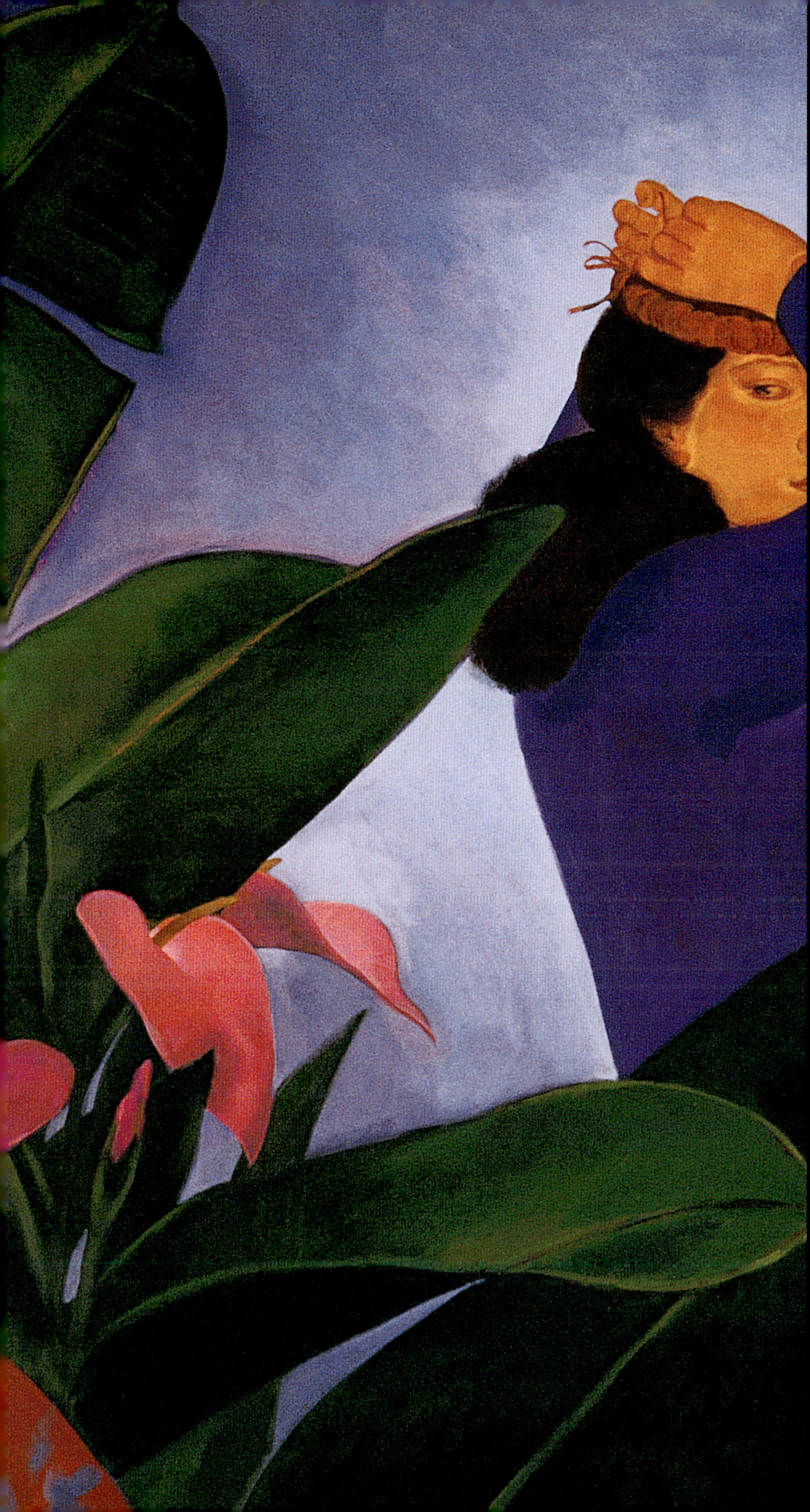

Na Kua Ana (sisters)
4 x 8 feet diptych, acrylic on canvas, 1992
Private collection

Untitled

2 x 4 feet, oil on canvas, 1982
Collection of the artist

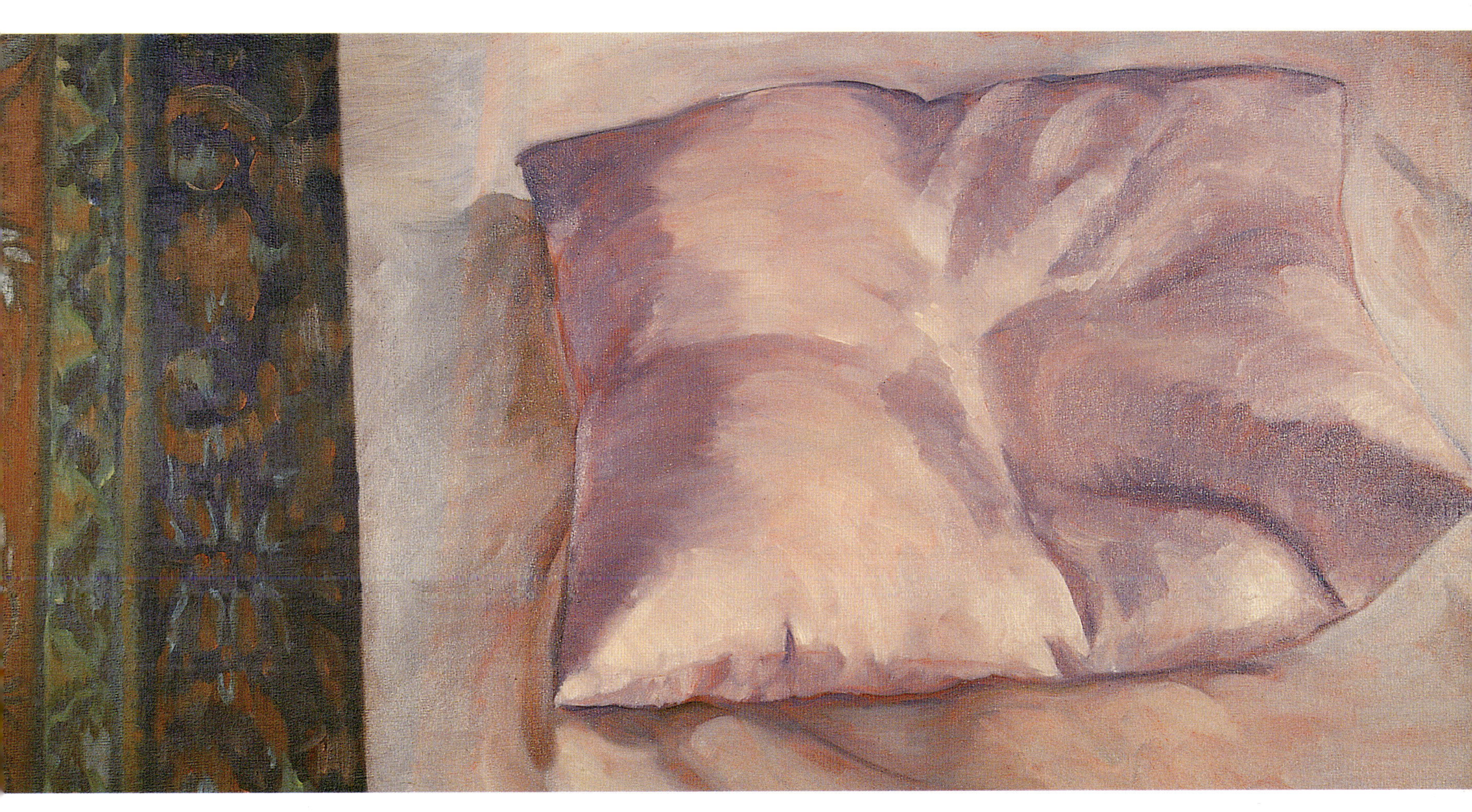

CLOUDS

Hawai`i has the most beautiful skies. One of my favorite sayings is "Beautiful skies are bread for the eyes." One could spend a lifetime painting nothing but the clouds over our ocean and mountains. Clouds evoke similar feelings in all of us, I think.

Ao (clouds)
4 x 4 feet, acrylic on canvas, 2001
Private collection

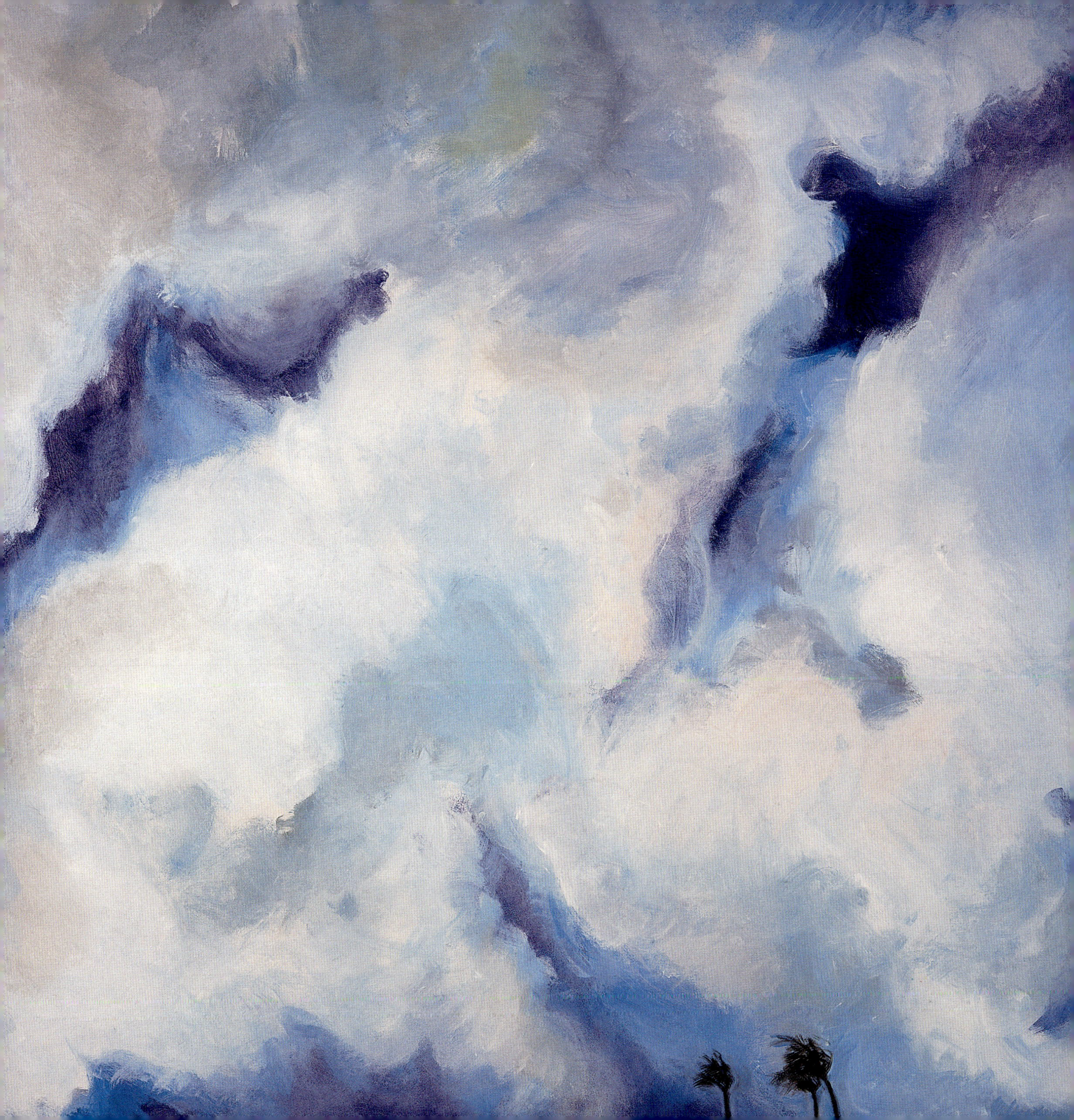

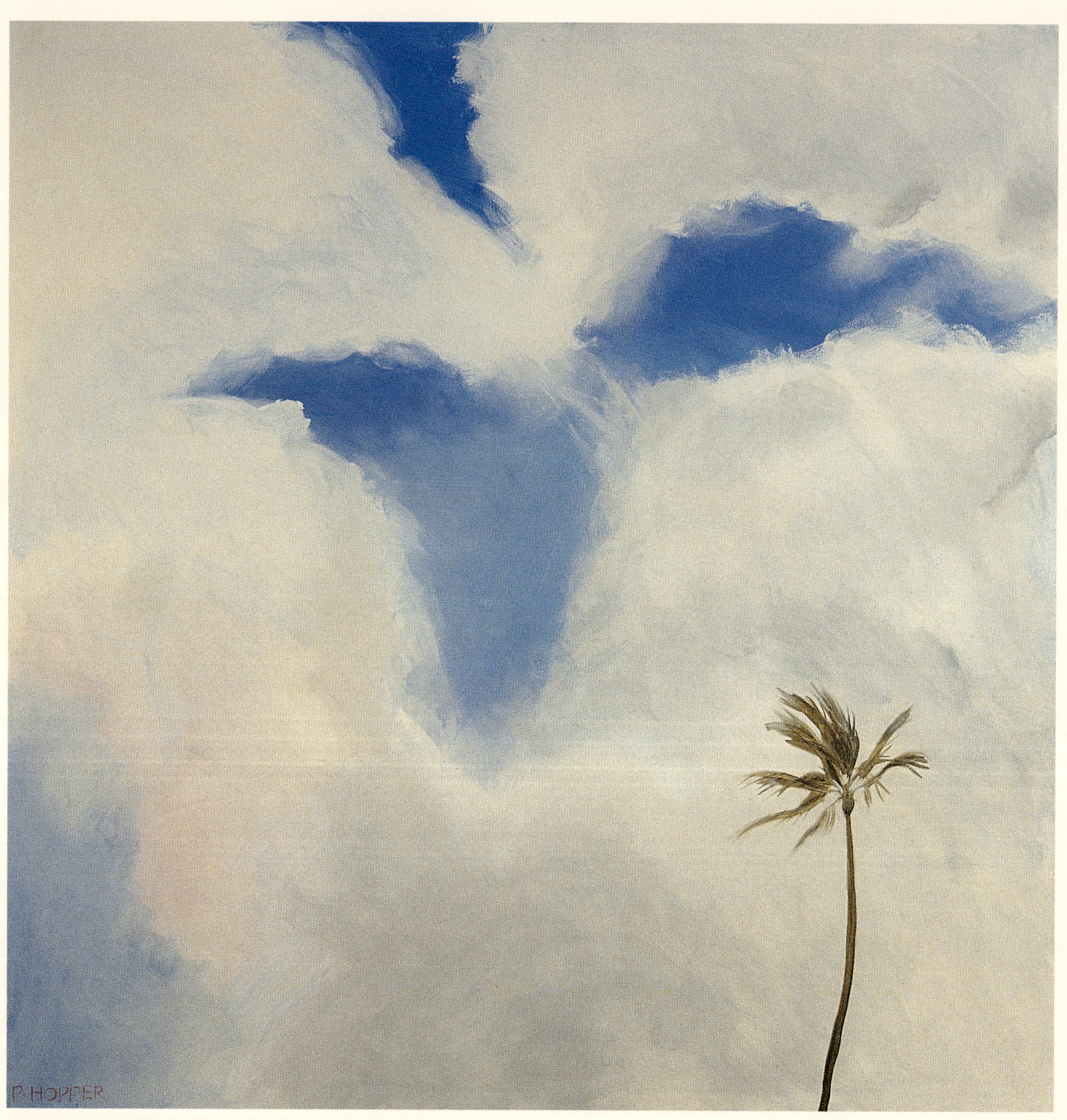
P. HOPPER

Ao II (clouds)
4 x 4 feet, acrylic on canvas, 2002
Pegge Hopper Gallery, Honolulu

Untitled

20 x 16 inches, acrylic on canvas, 2002

Pegge Hopper Gallery, Honolulu

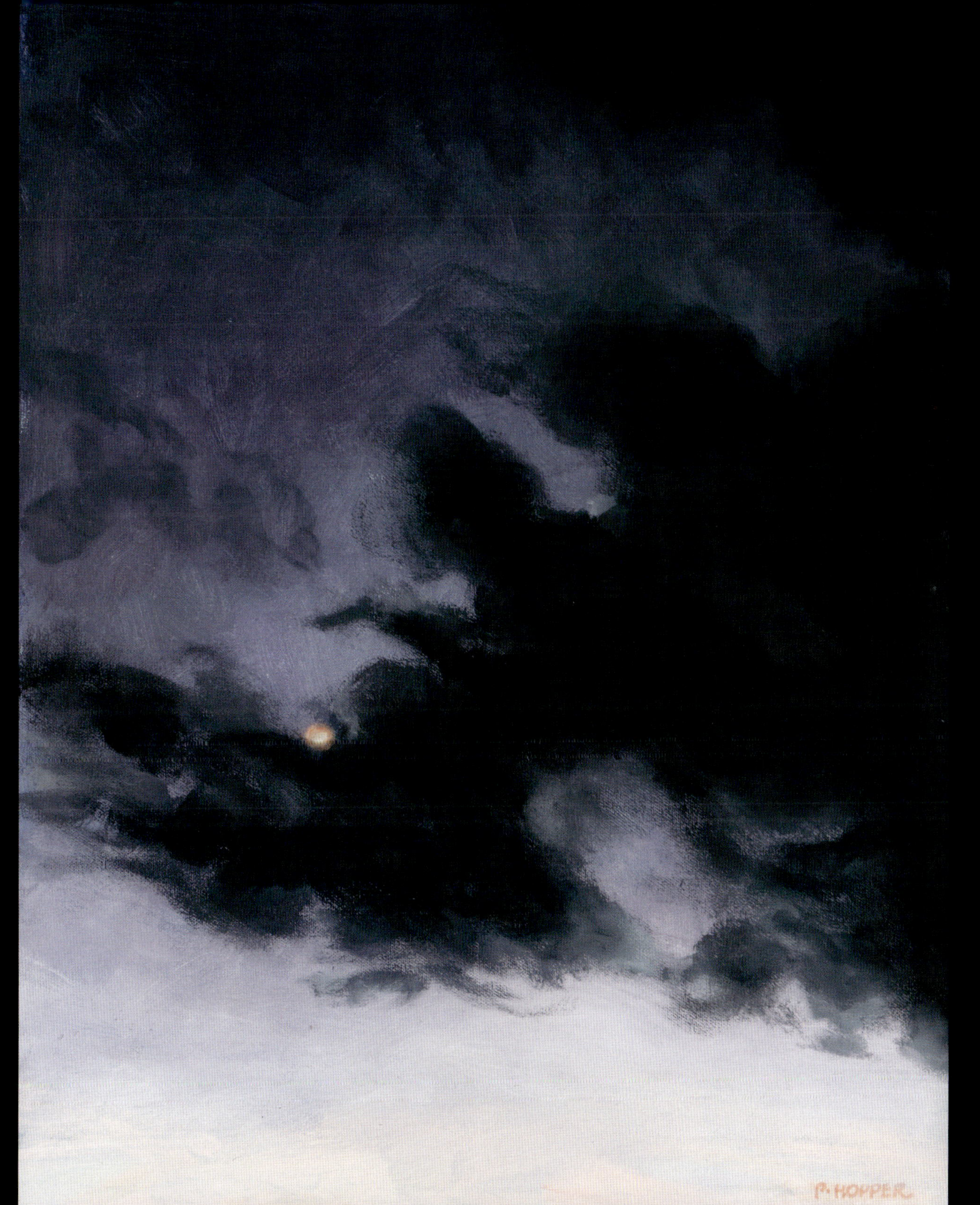
P. HOPPER

THE FIVE ELEMENTS

A wonderful Eurasian restaurant, Indigo, opened down the street from my gallery and the wife of the chef asked me to do a series of paintings based on the five elements of Chinese cooking: fire, water, wood, earth, and metal. She gave me a fabulous book of old Chinese costumes. It inspired me to pick costumes that I thought expressed each element.

Fire
8 x 4 feet, acrylic and pastel on board, 1996
Pegge Hopper Gallery, Honolulu

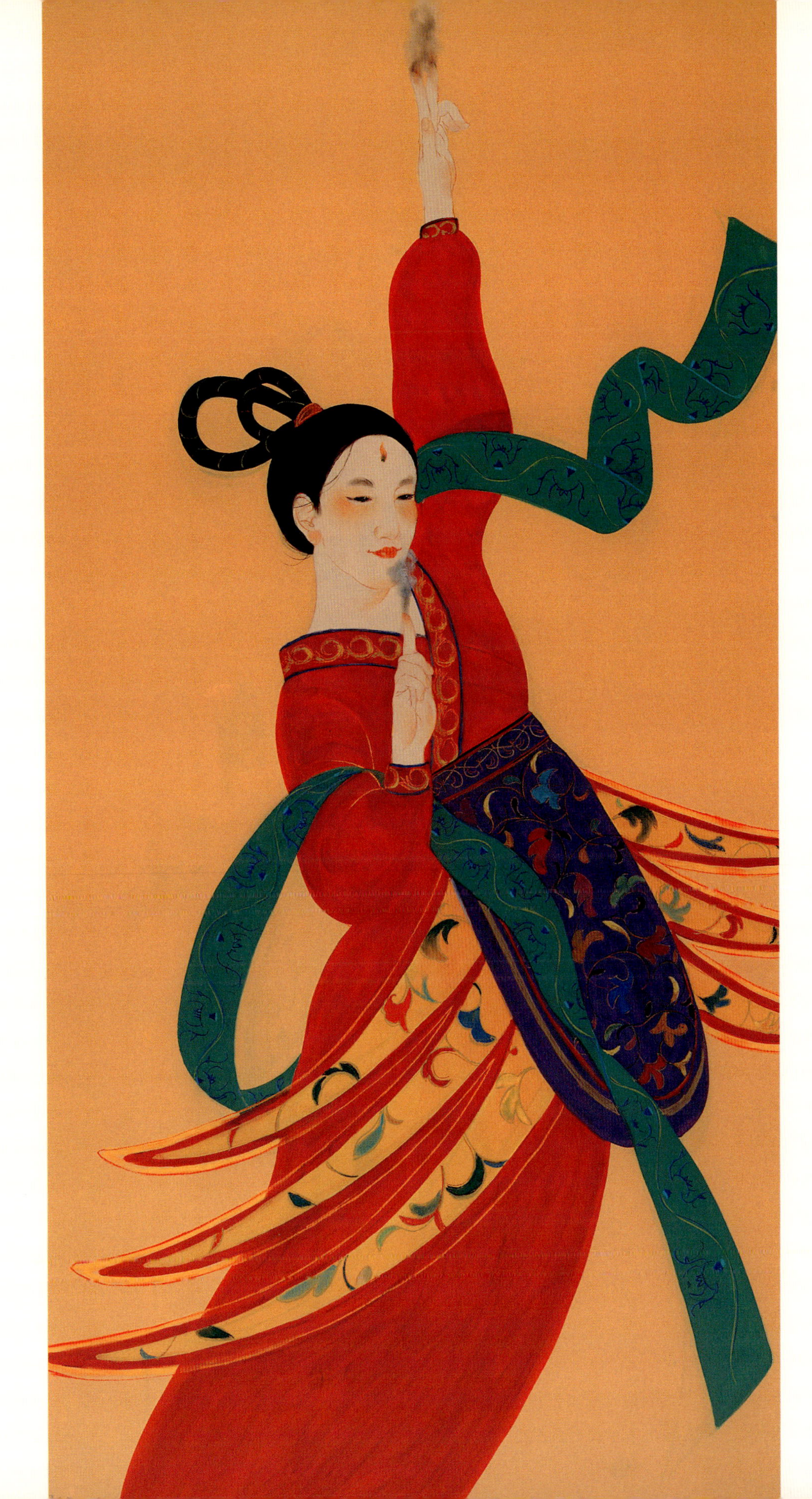

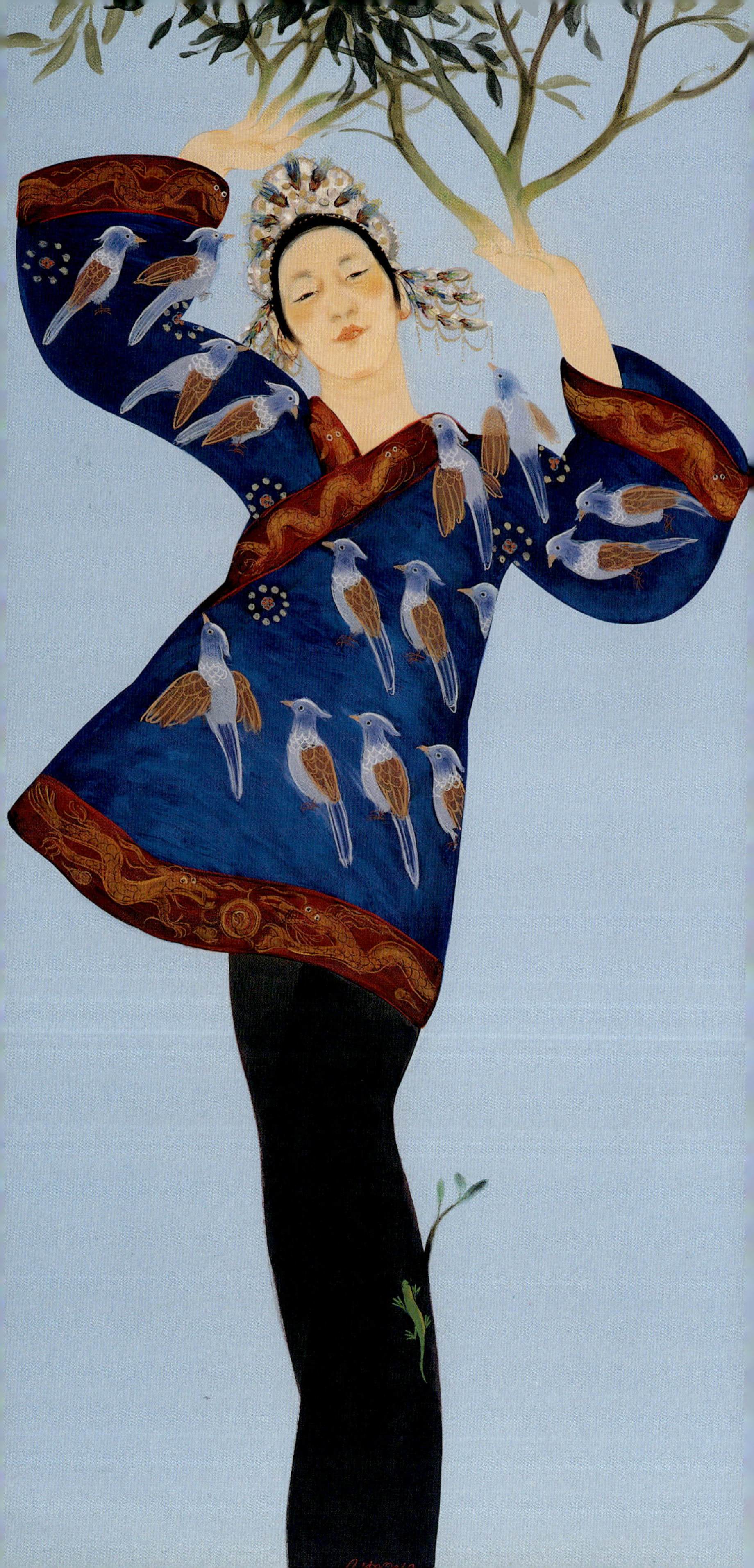

Wood
8 x 4 feet, acrylic and pastel on board, 1996
Pegge Hopper Gallery, Honolulu

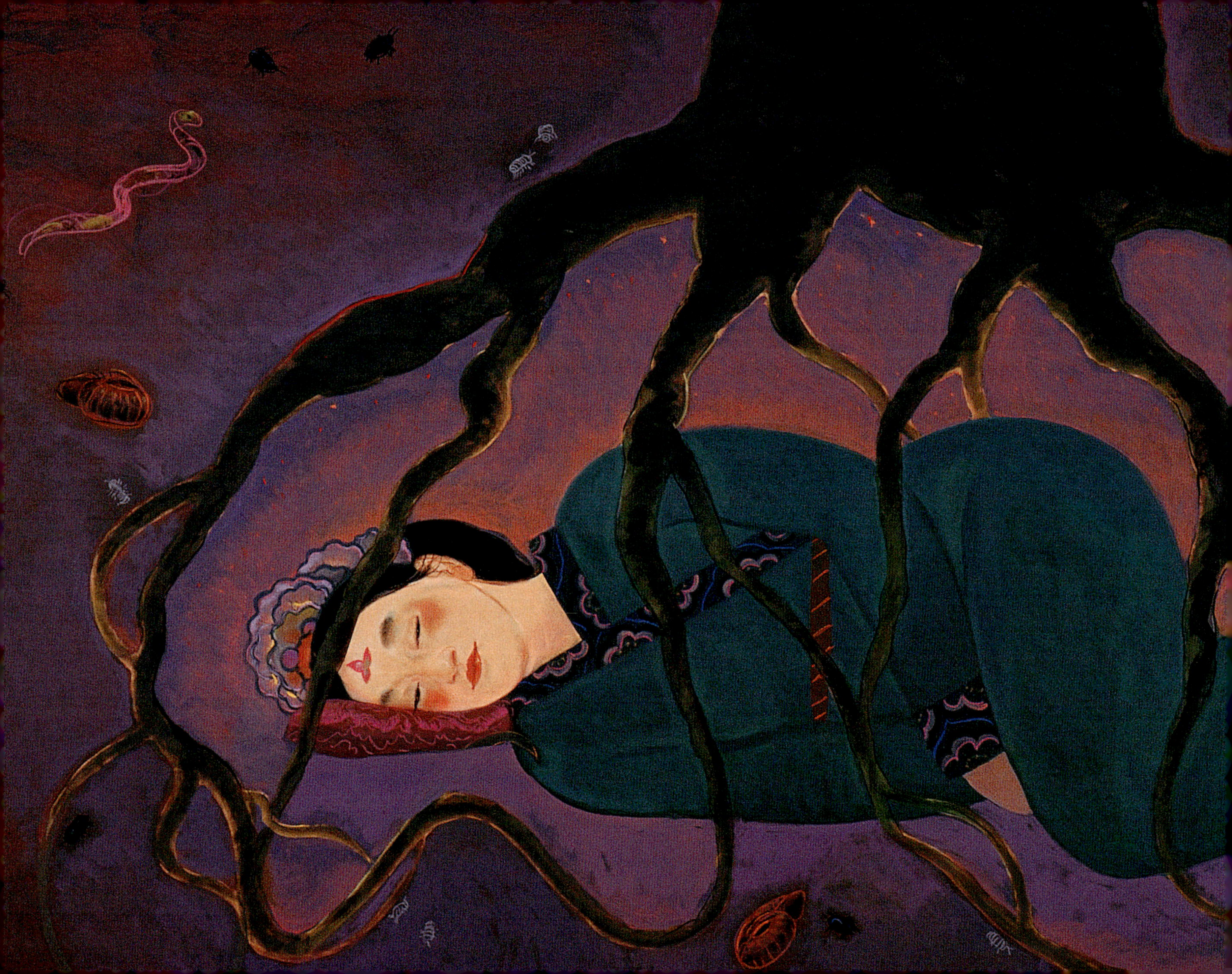

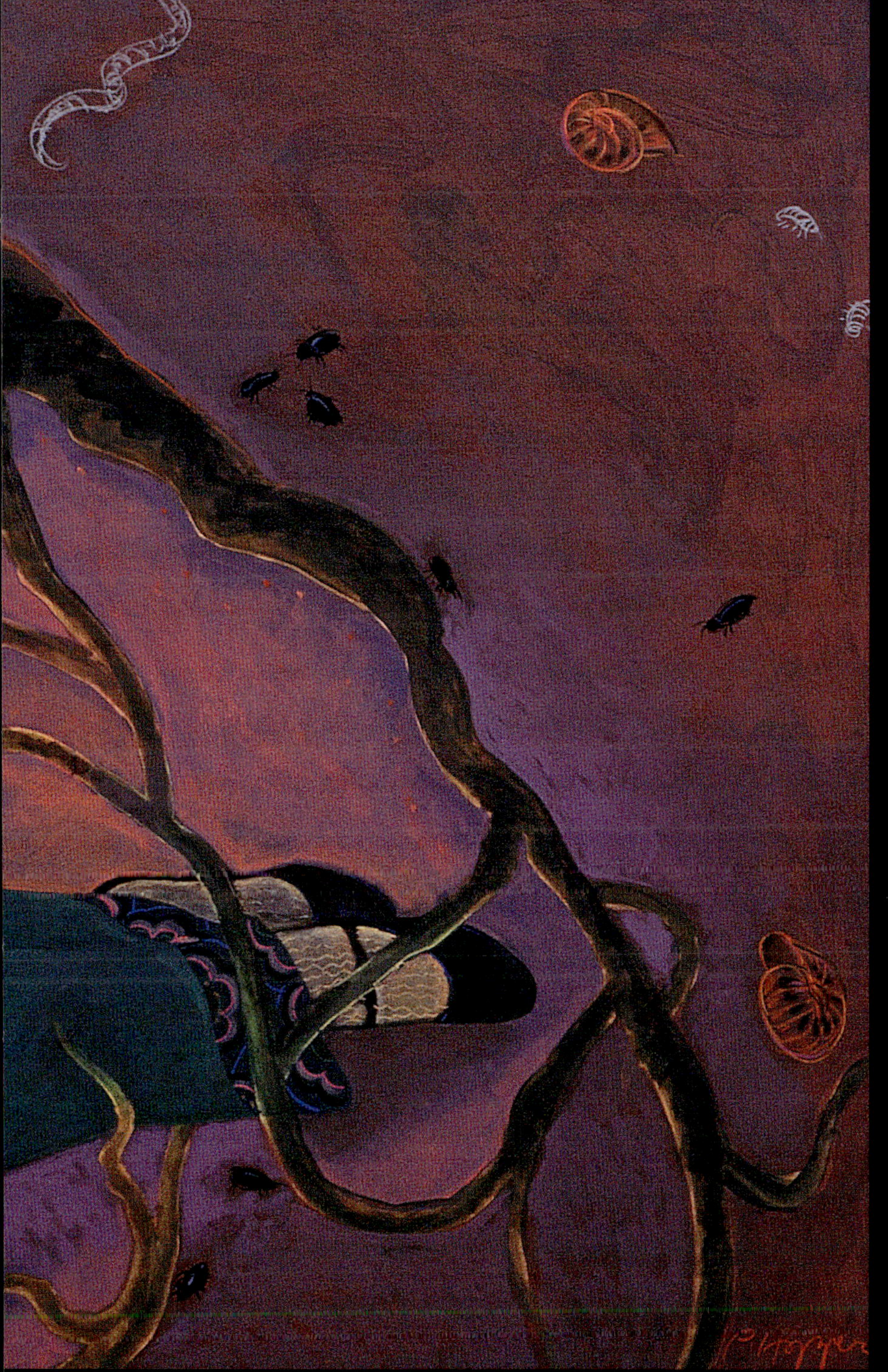

Earth
4 x 8 feet, acrylic and pastel on board,
Pegge Hopper Gallery, Honolulu

{OVERLEAF} *Water*
4 x 8 feet, acrylic and pastel on board,
Pegge Hopper Gallery, Honolulu

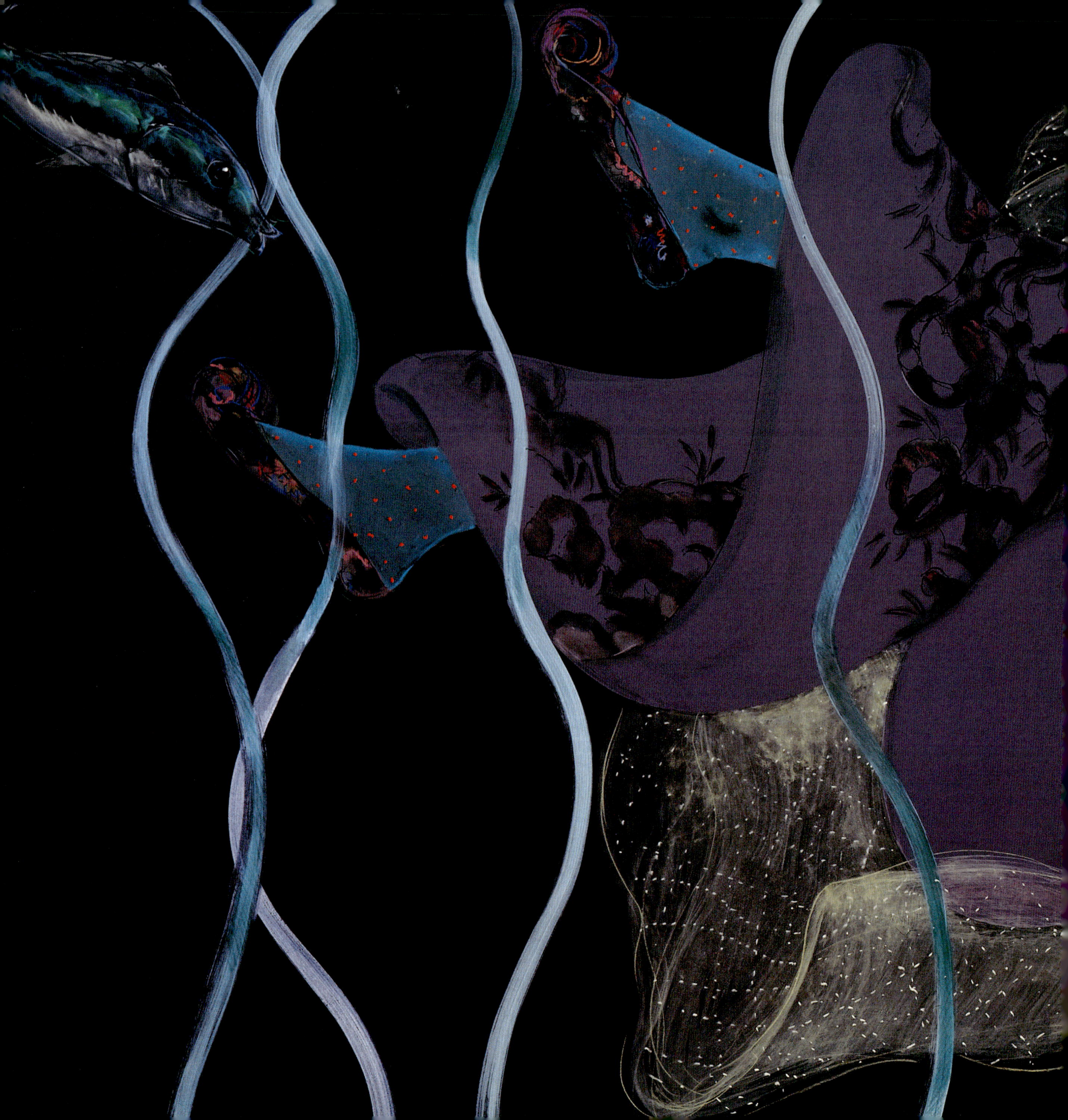

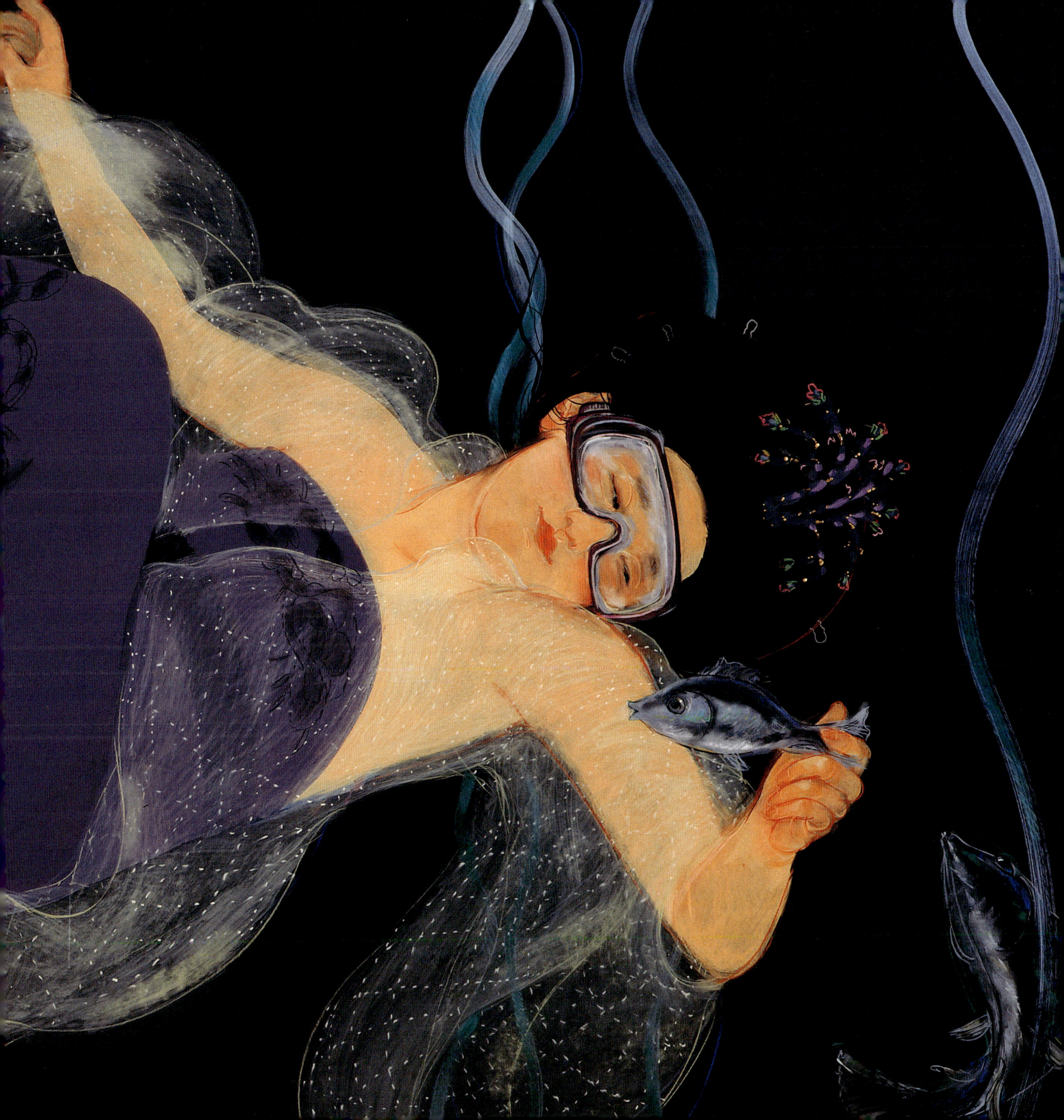

Metal

8 x 4 feet, acrylic and pastel on board, 1996
Pegge Hopper Gallery, Honolulu

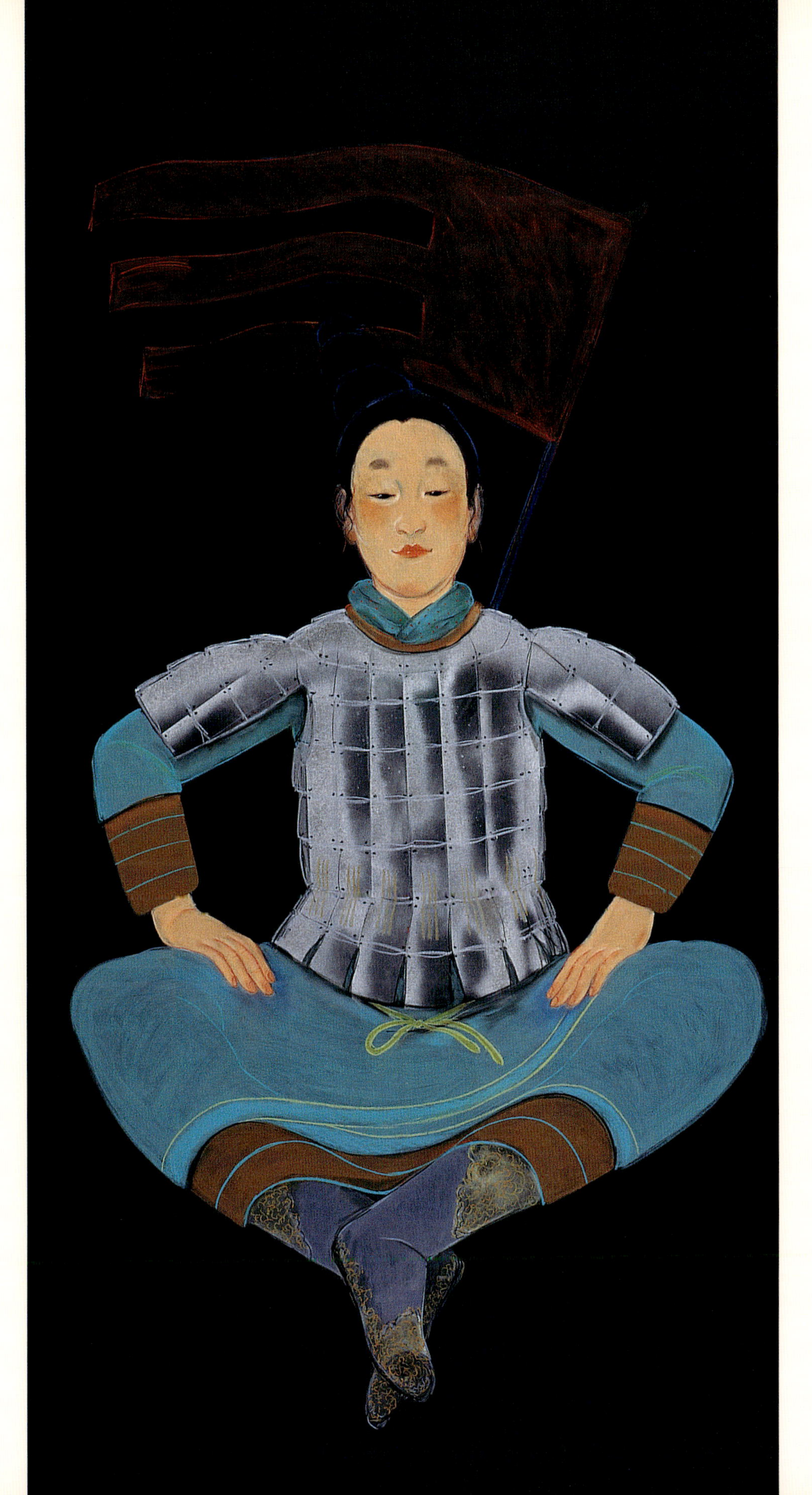

SWIMMING

These paintings have a very practical beginning. My pool needed to be retiled and the contractor wanted to trade his services for art work. What better image for a pool man than water? He liked the painting and I liked doing it, so I did a few more. Water is such a part of our life in Hawai`i, and I love swimming and snorkeling.

Mana`olana (floating thoughts)
5 x 5 feet, acrylic on canvas, 1990
Private collection

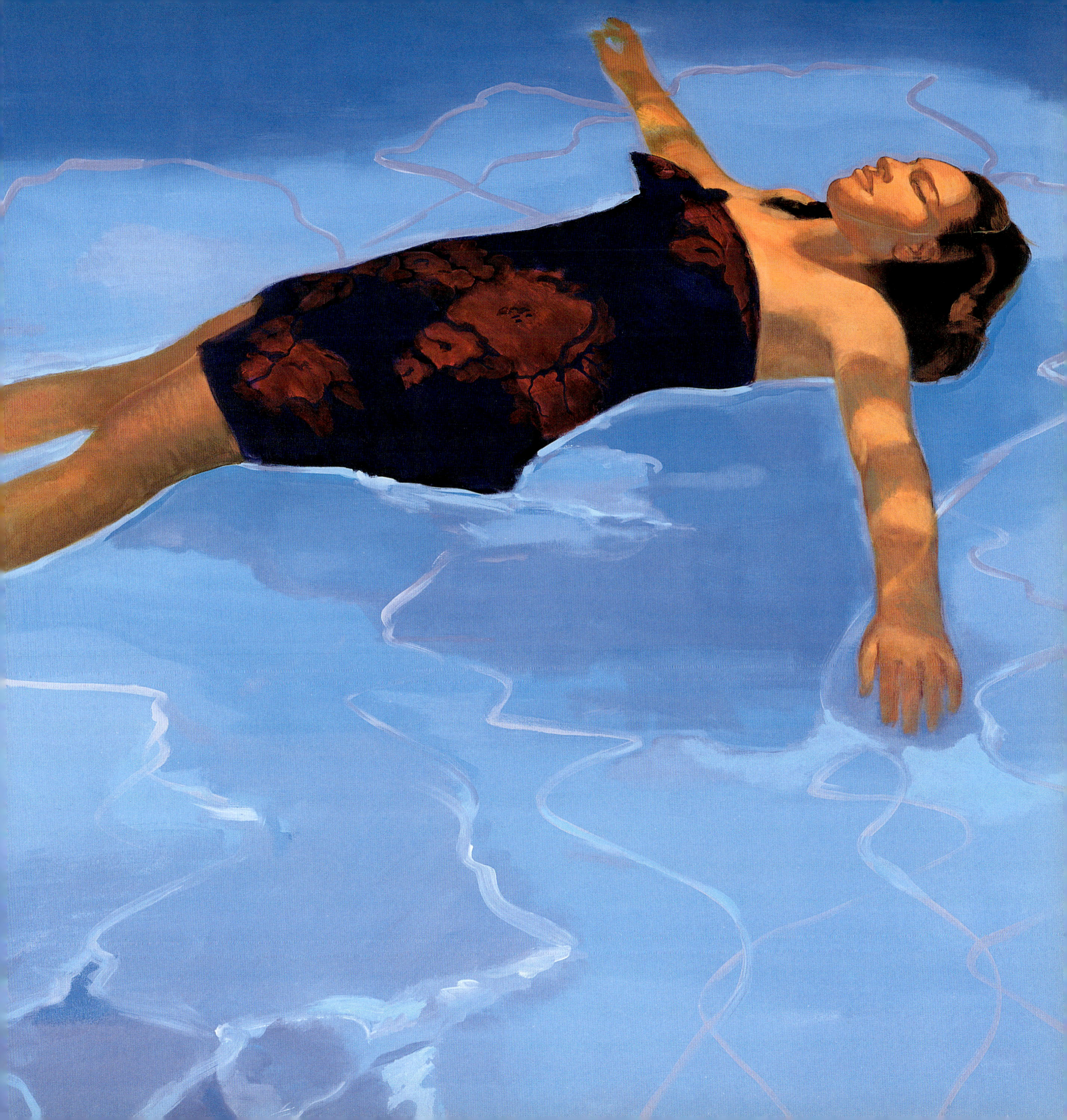

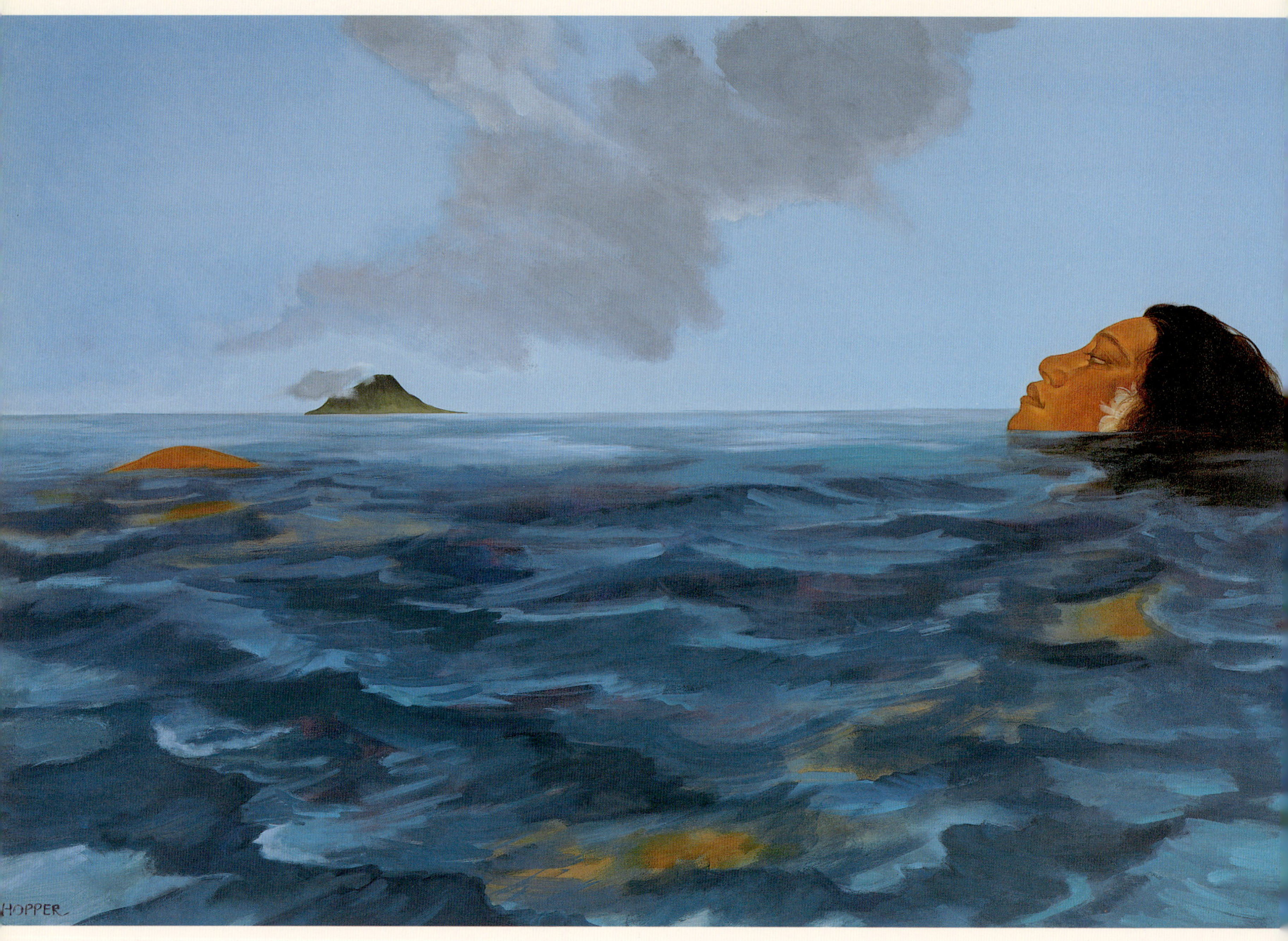
HOPPER

{OPPOSITE} *Untitled*
4 x 6 feet, acrylic on canvas, 1989
Private collection

Ho`olewa
2 x 6 feet, acrylic on canvas, 1989
Private collection

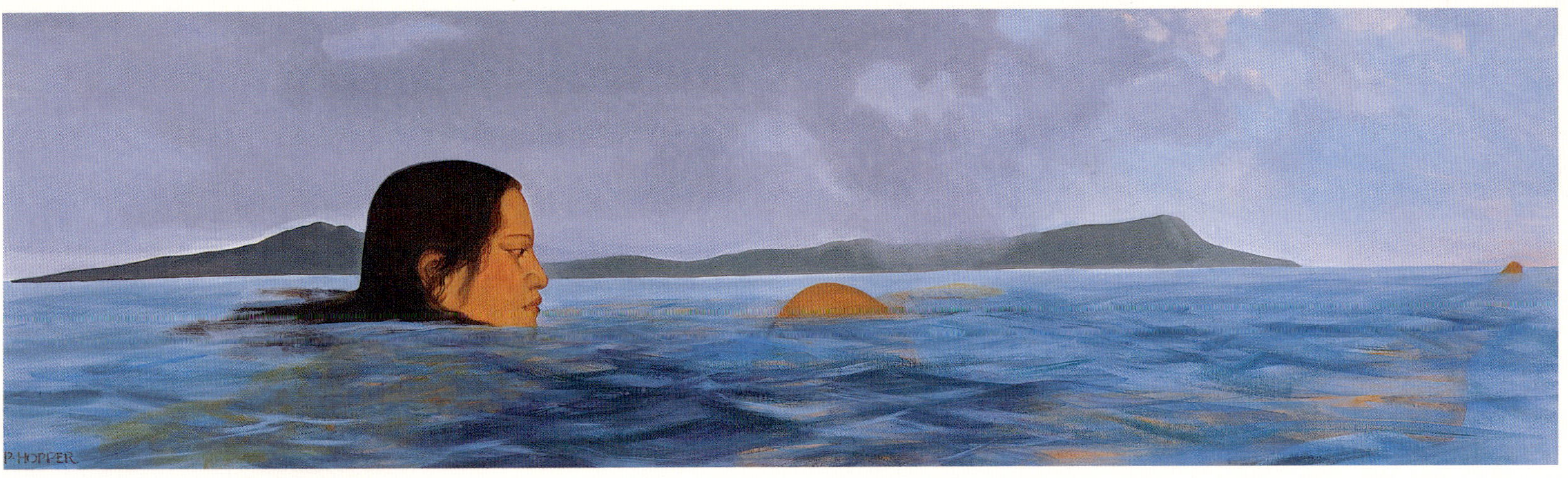

Elly Swimming
74 3 x 4 feet, acrylic on board, 1998
Collection of the artist

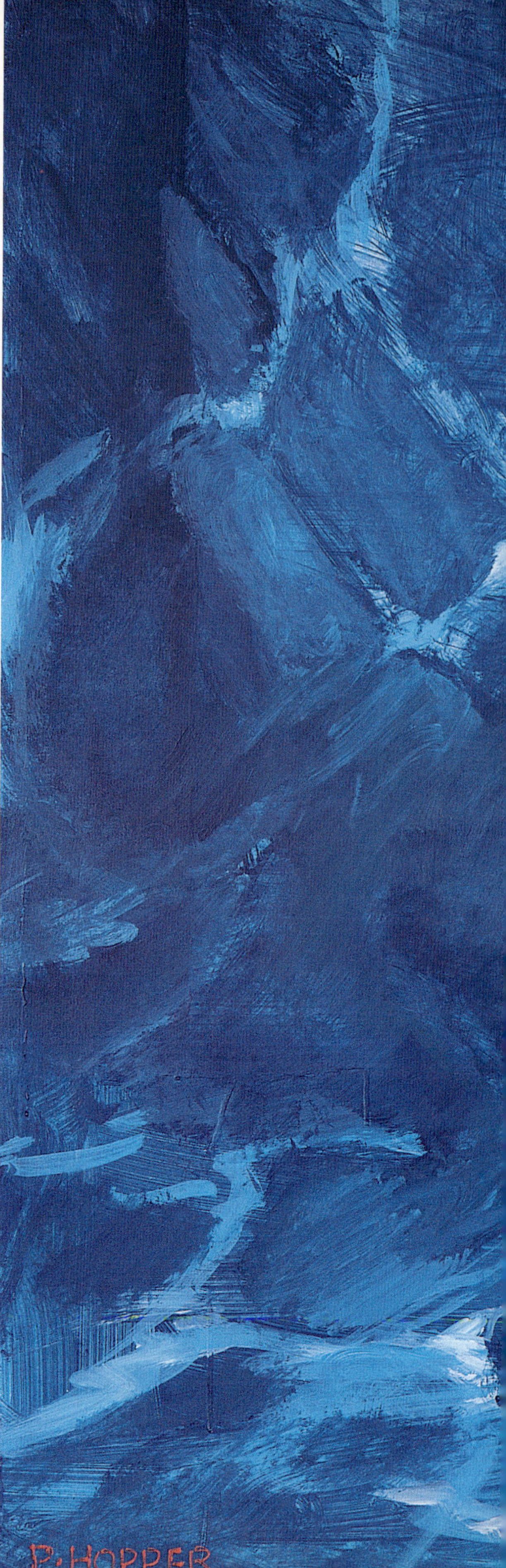

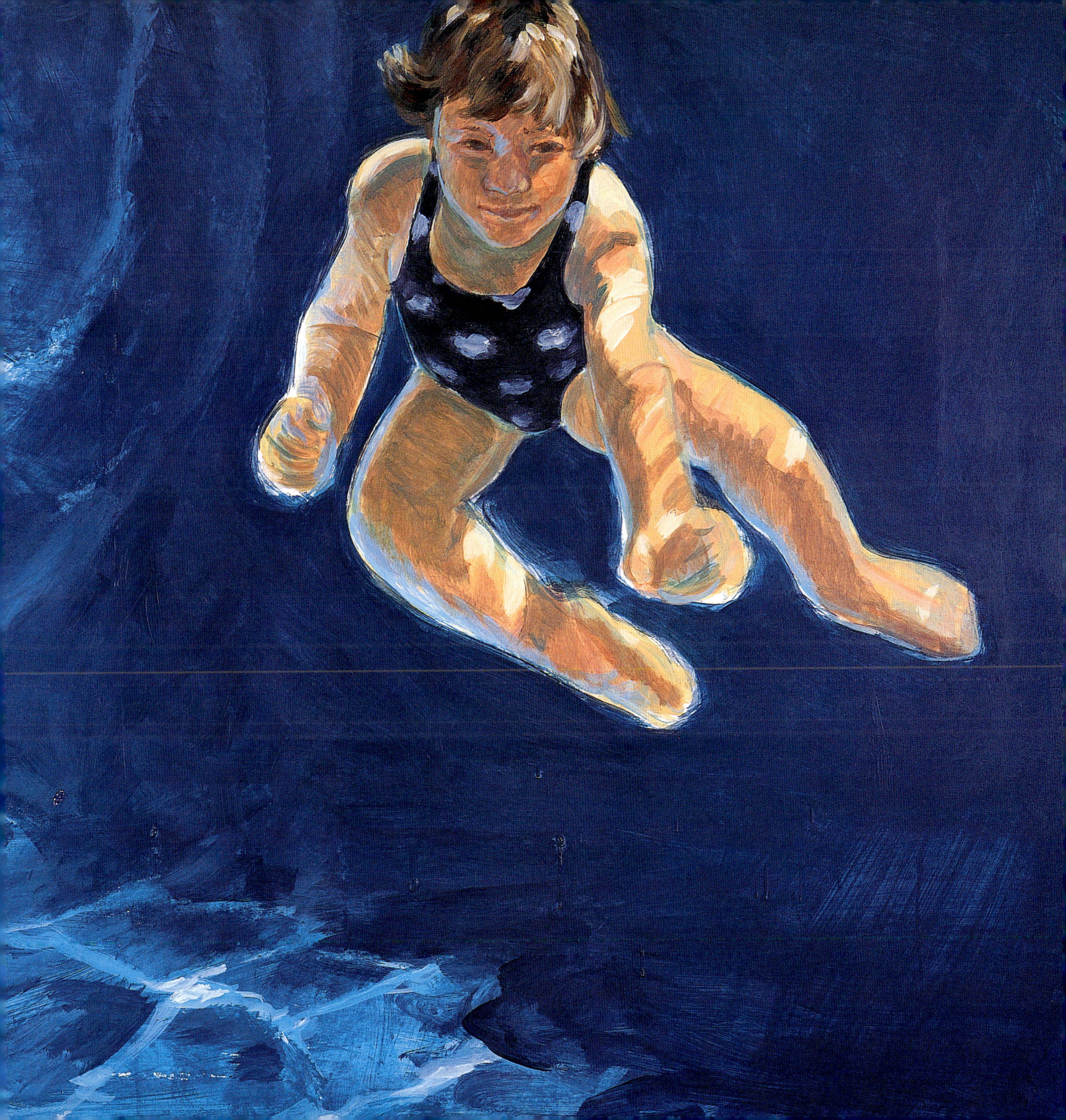

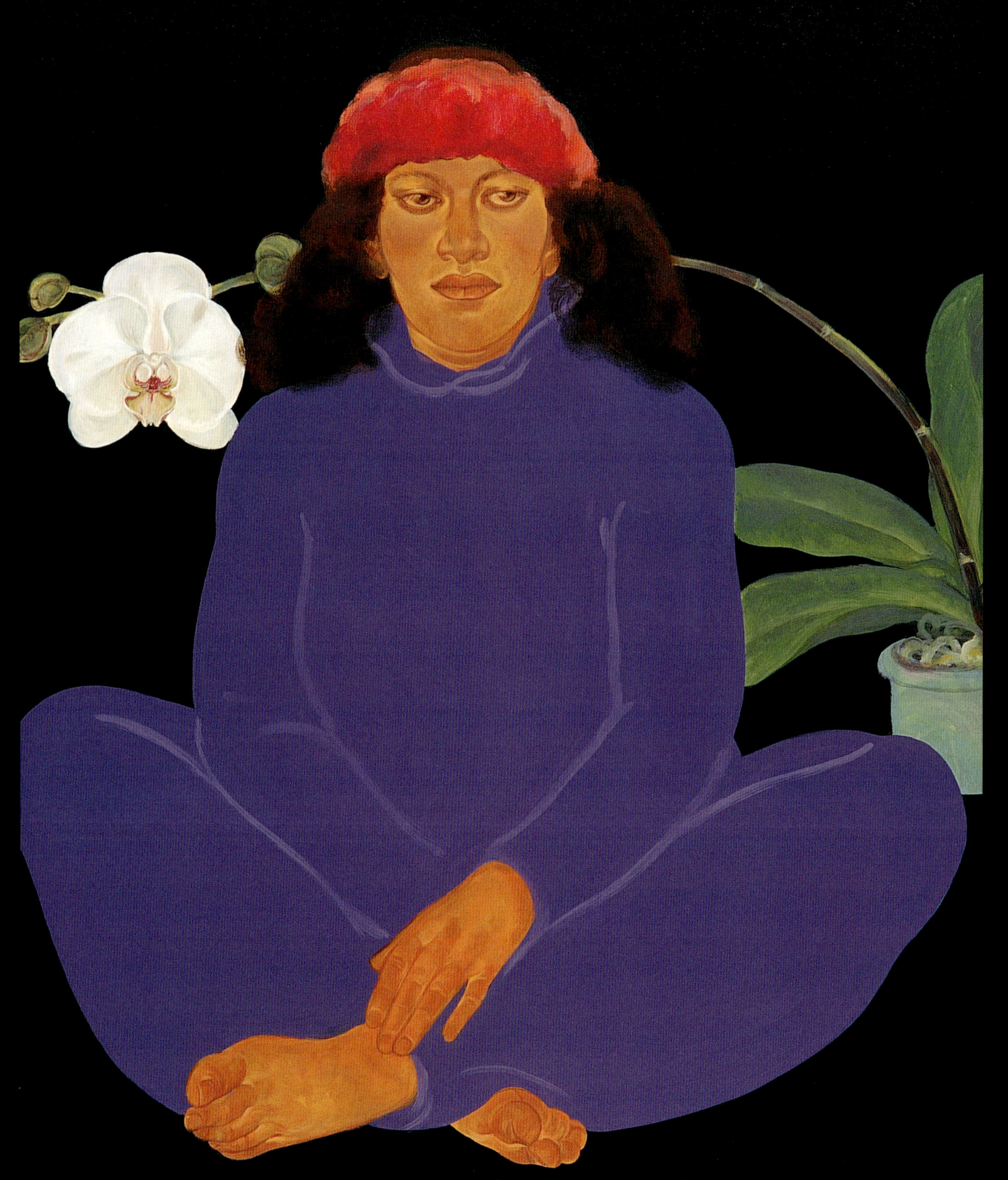
P. HOPPER

Okika
4 x 3 feet, acrylic on canvas, 2001
Napua Gallery, Maui

Palama

40 x 30 inches, acrylic on canvas, 2001
Napua Gallery, Maui

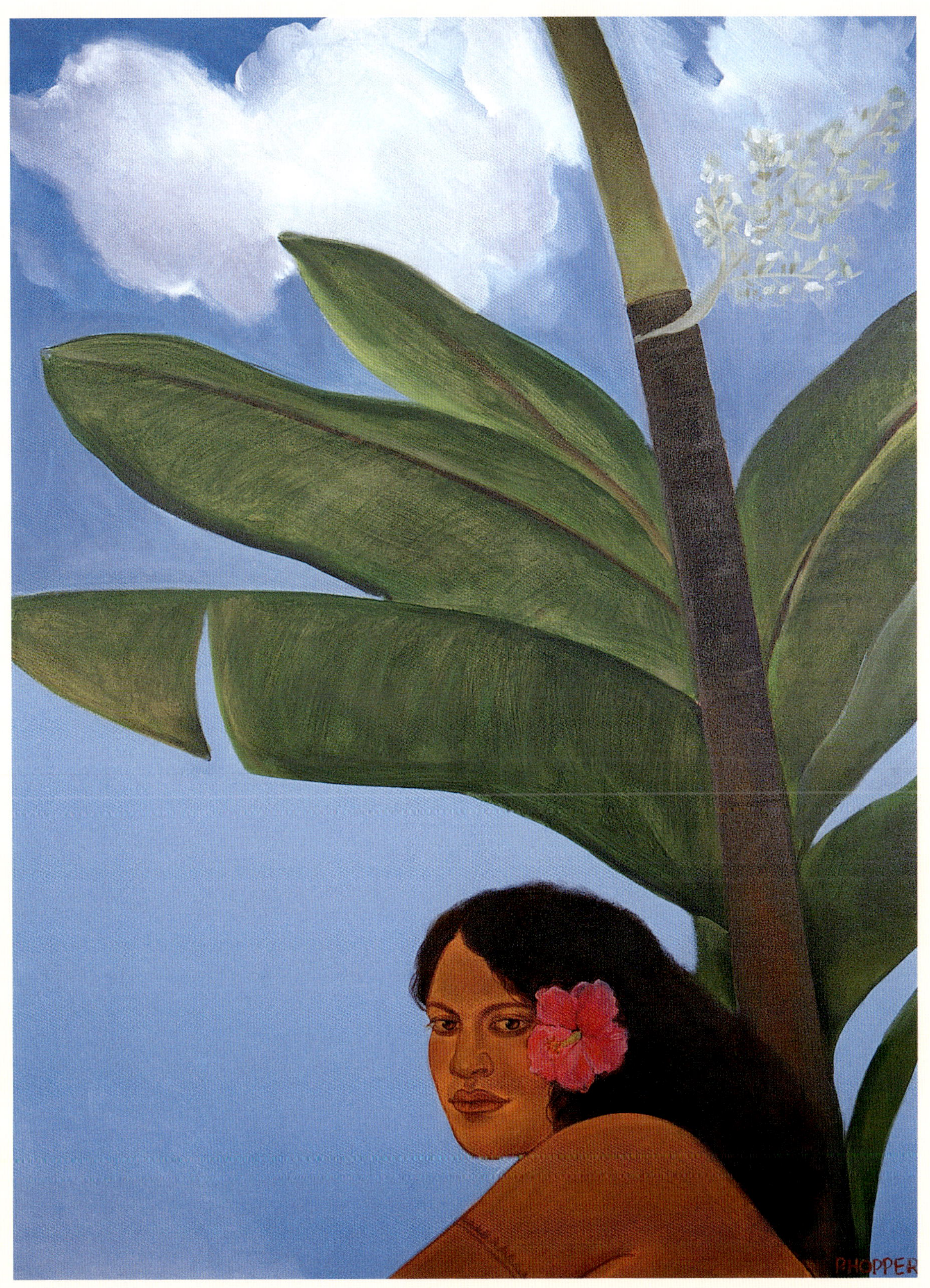
PHOPPER

Antherium

3 x 2 feet, acrylic on canvas, 2000

Pegge Hopper Gallery, Honolulu

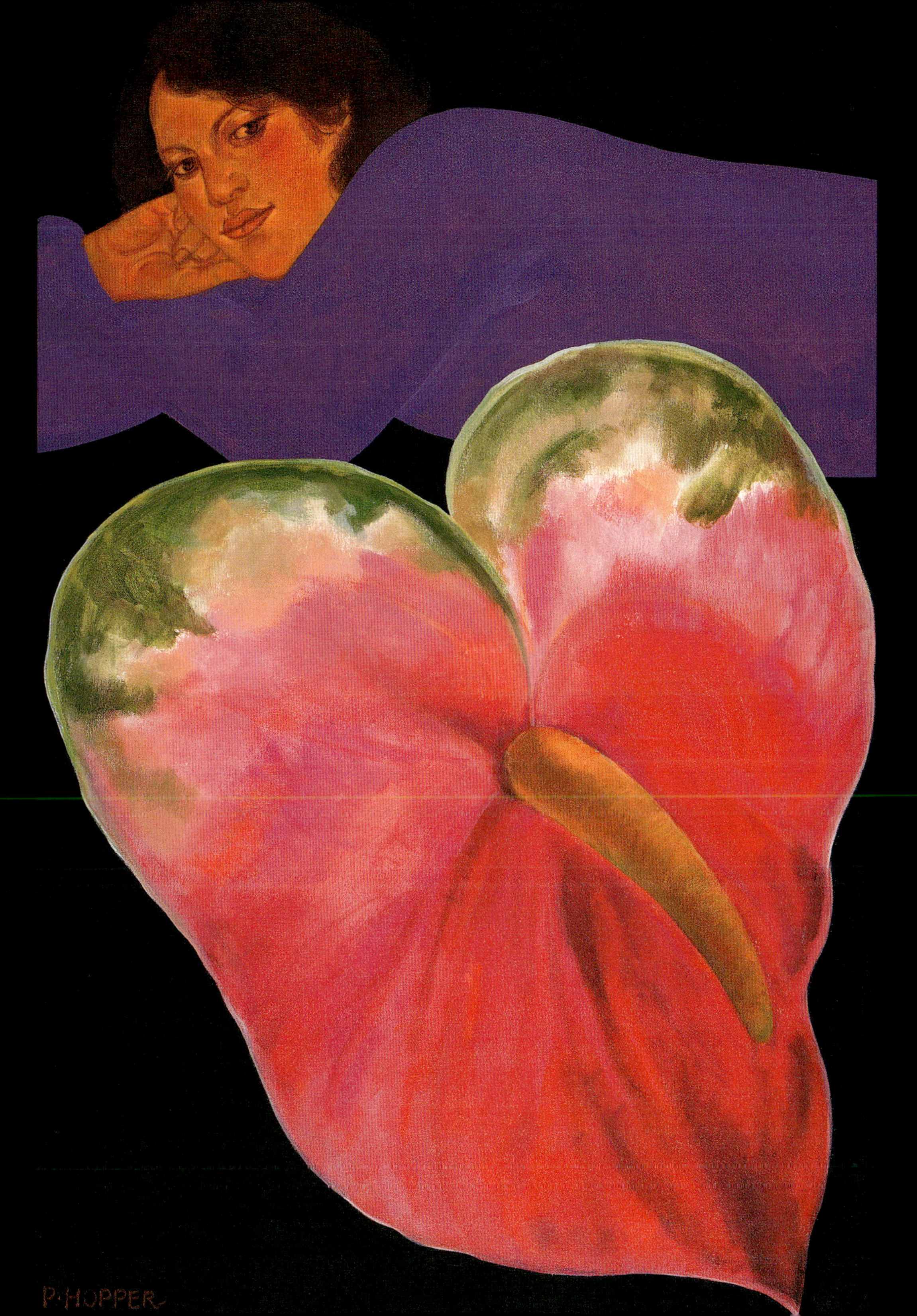
P·HOPPER

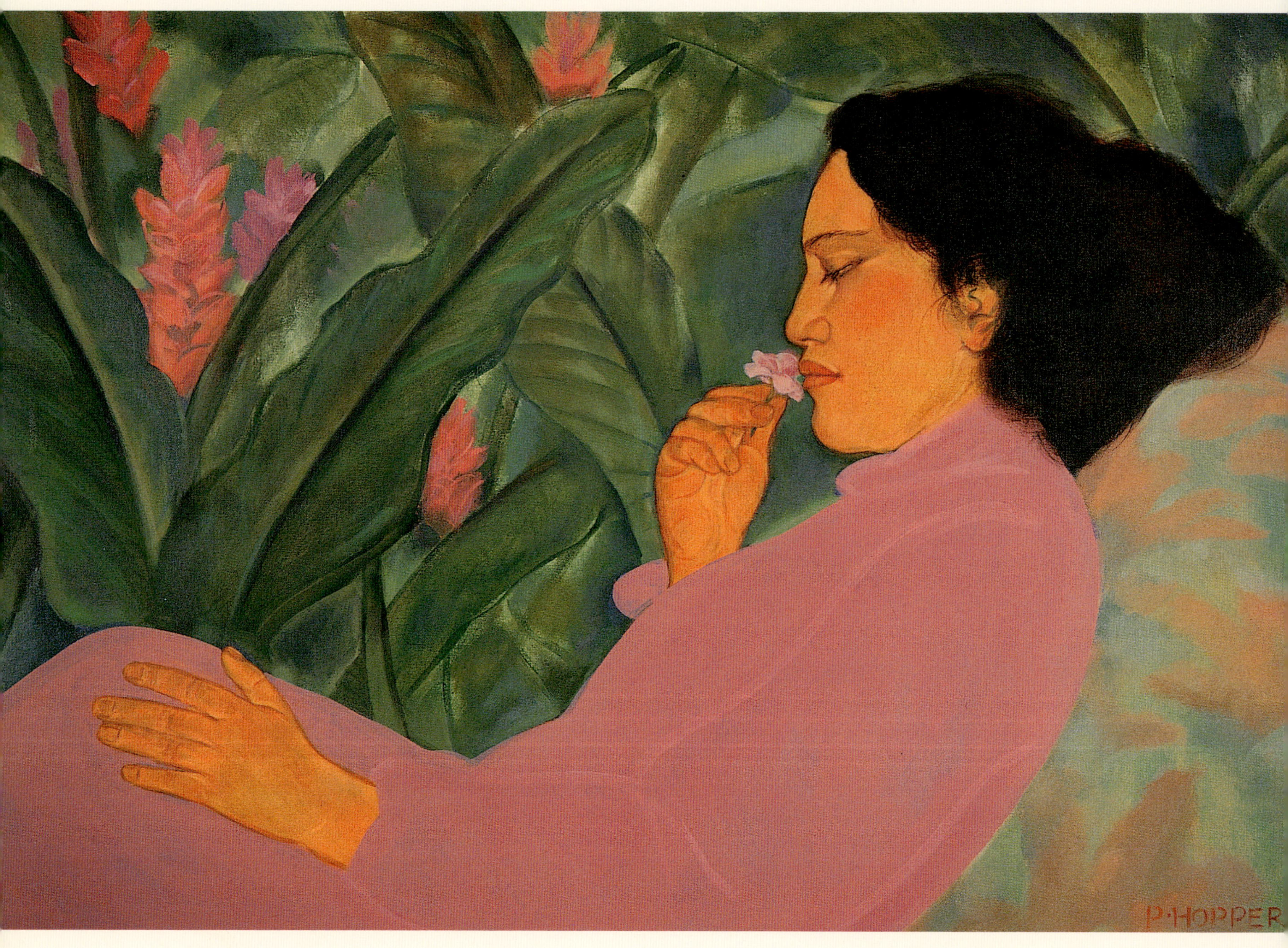
P·HOPPER

A'ala
2 x 3 feet, acrylic on canvas, 2001
Private collection

Yellow Ginger
6 x 4 feet, acrylic on canvas, 1994
Private collection

{OPPOSITE} *Hanging Helicona*
30 x 40 inches, acrylic on canvas, 2000
Pegge Hopper Gallery, Honolulu

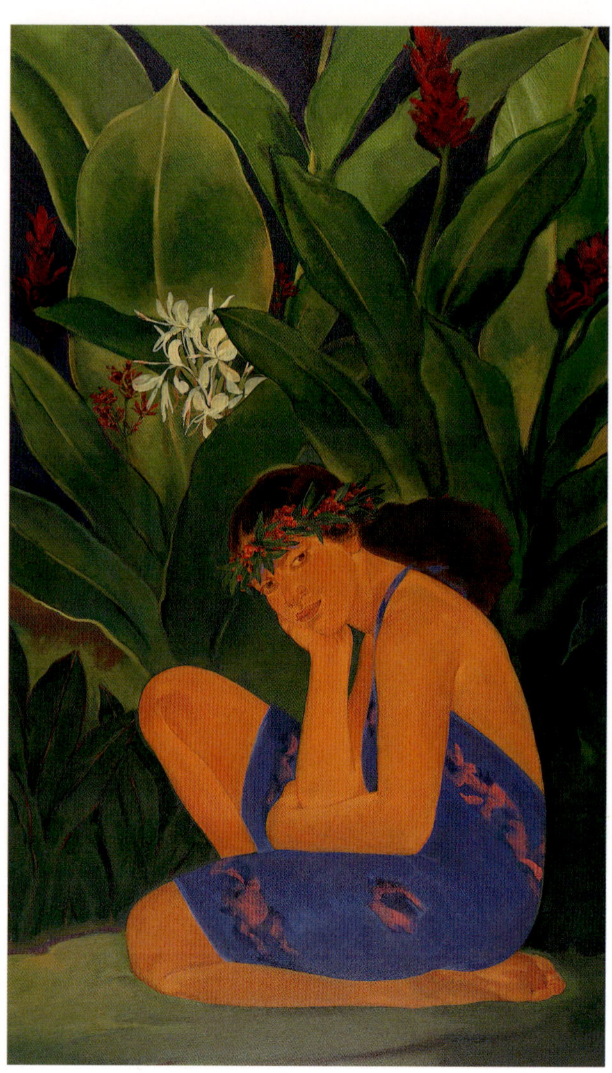

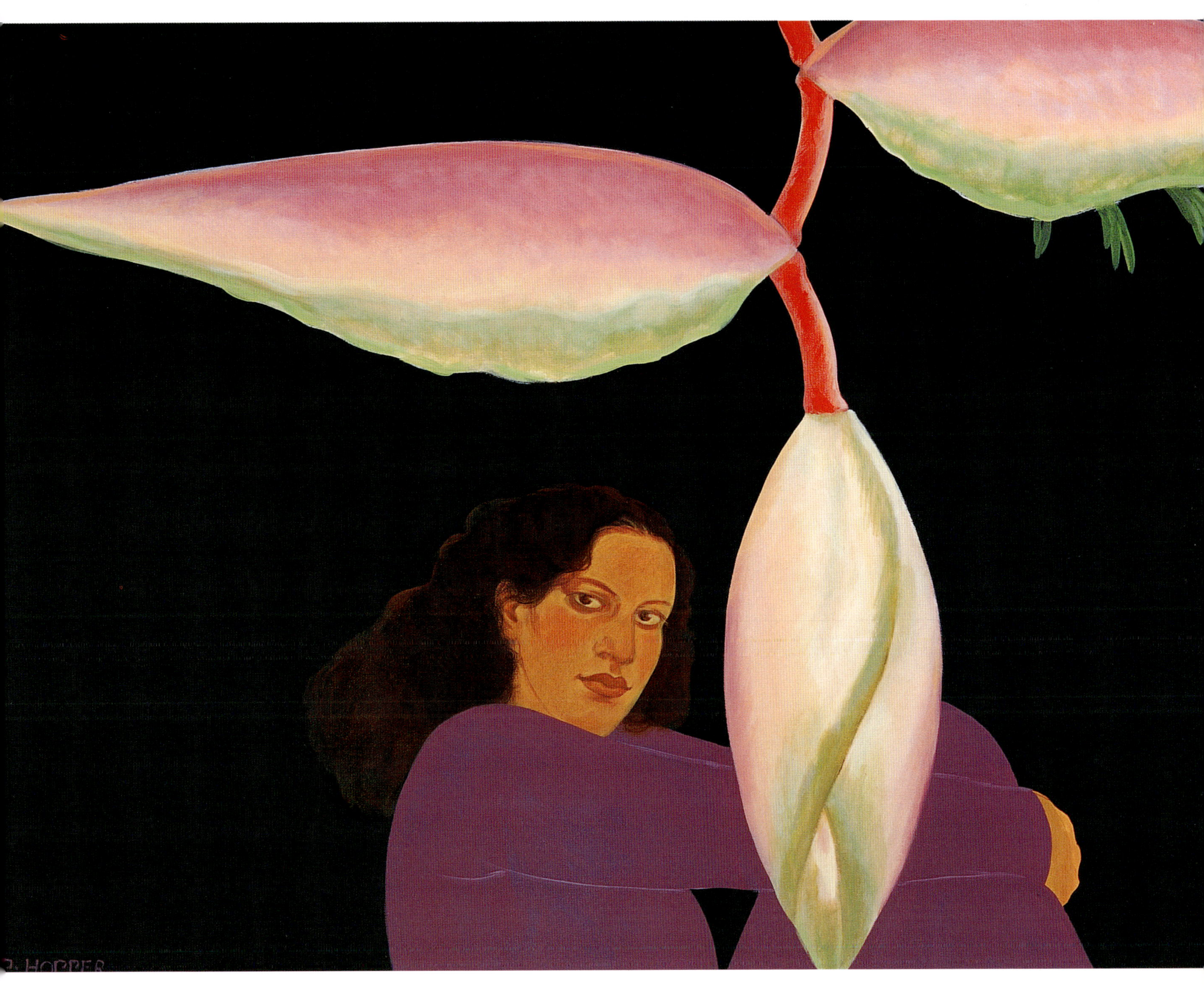

Okika

86 2 x 3 feet, acrylic on canvas, 2000

Pegge Hopper Gallery, Honolulu

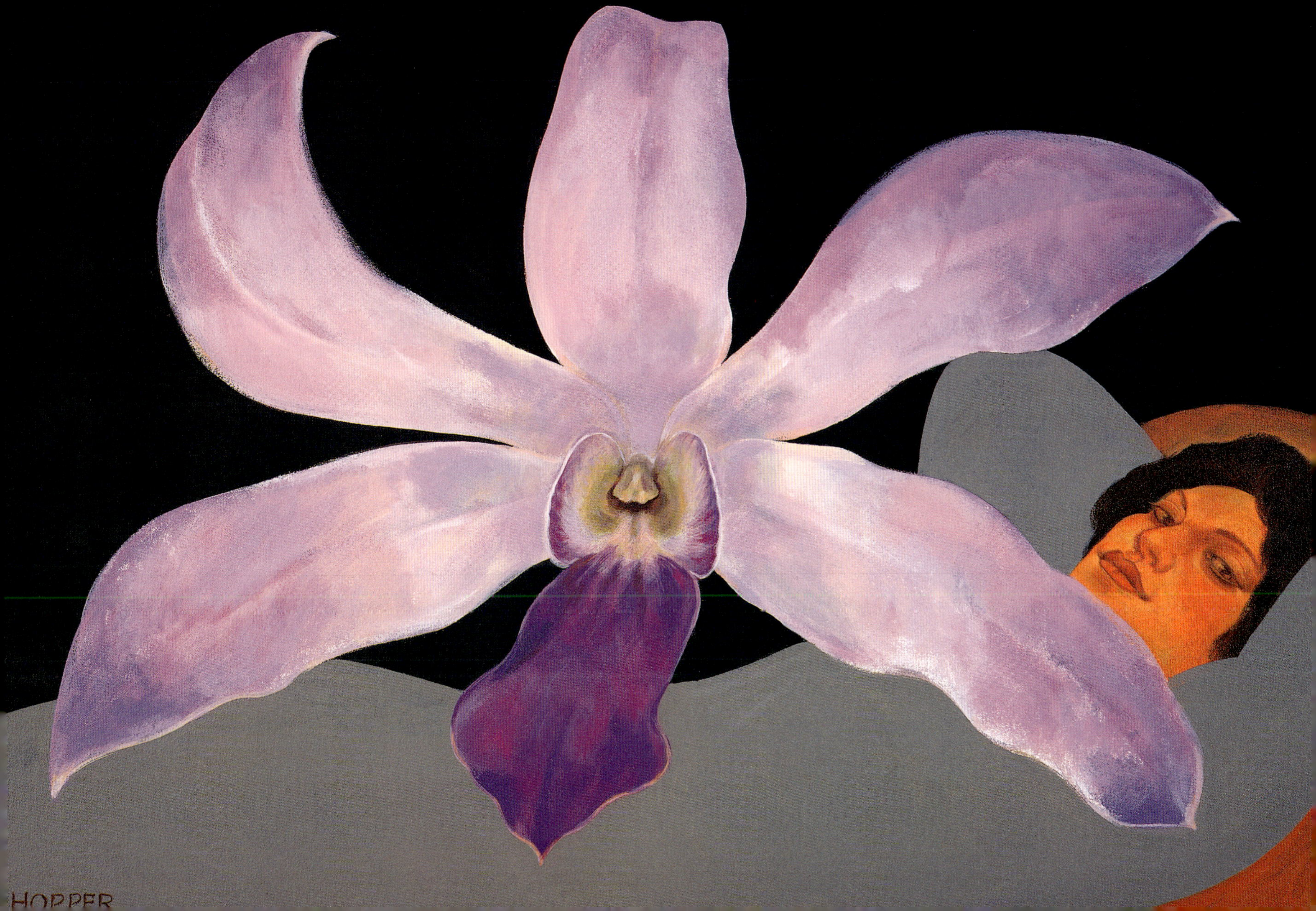
HOPPER

Otahiti
4 x 6 feet, acrylic on canvas, 1986
Private collection

{OVERLEAF} *Kapalua*
4 x 10 feet, acrylic on canvas, 1998
Private collection

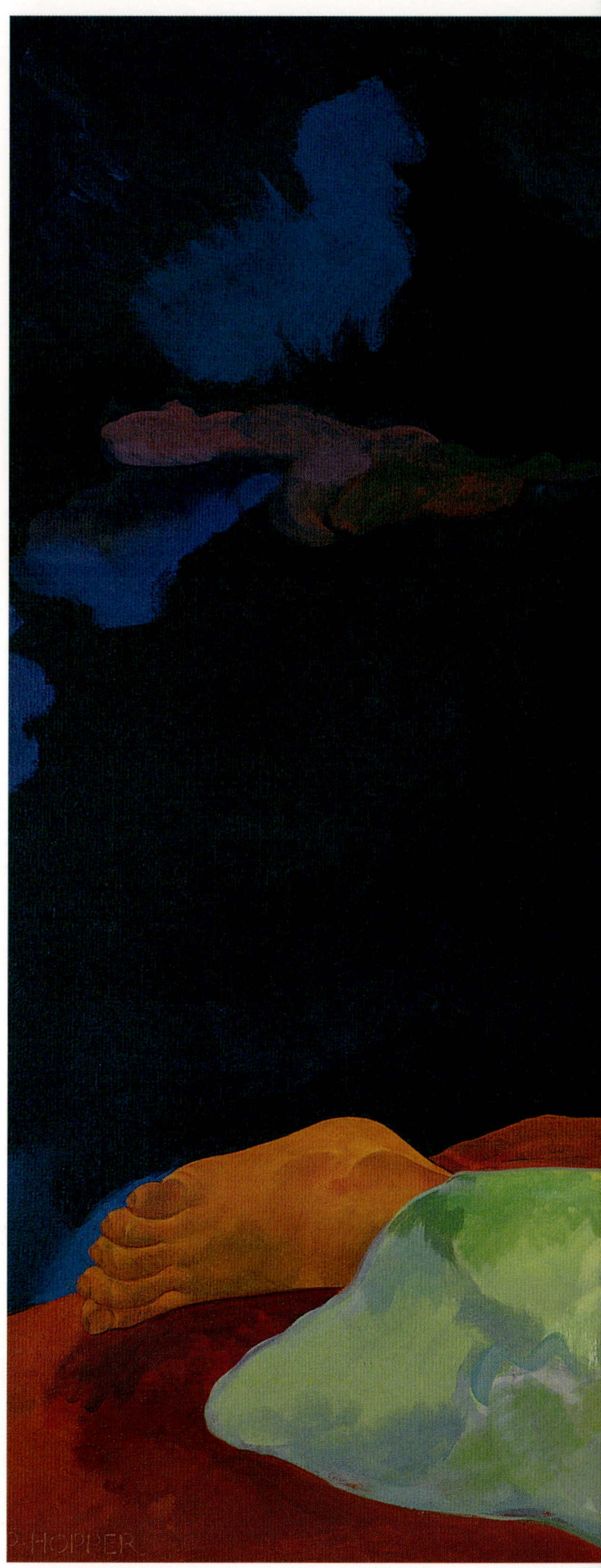

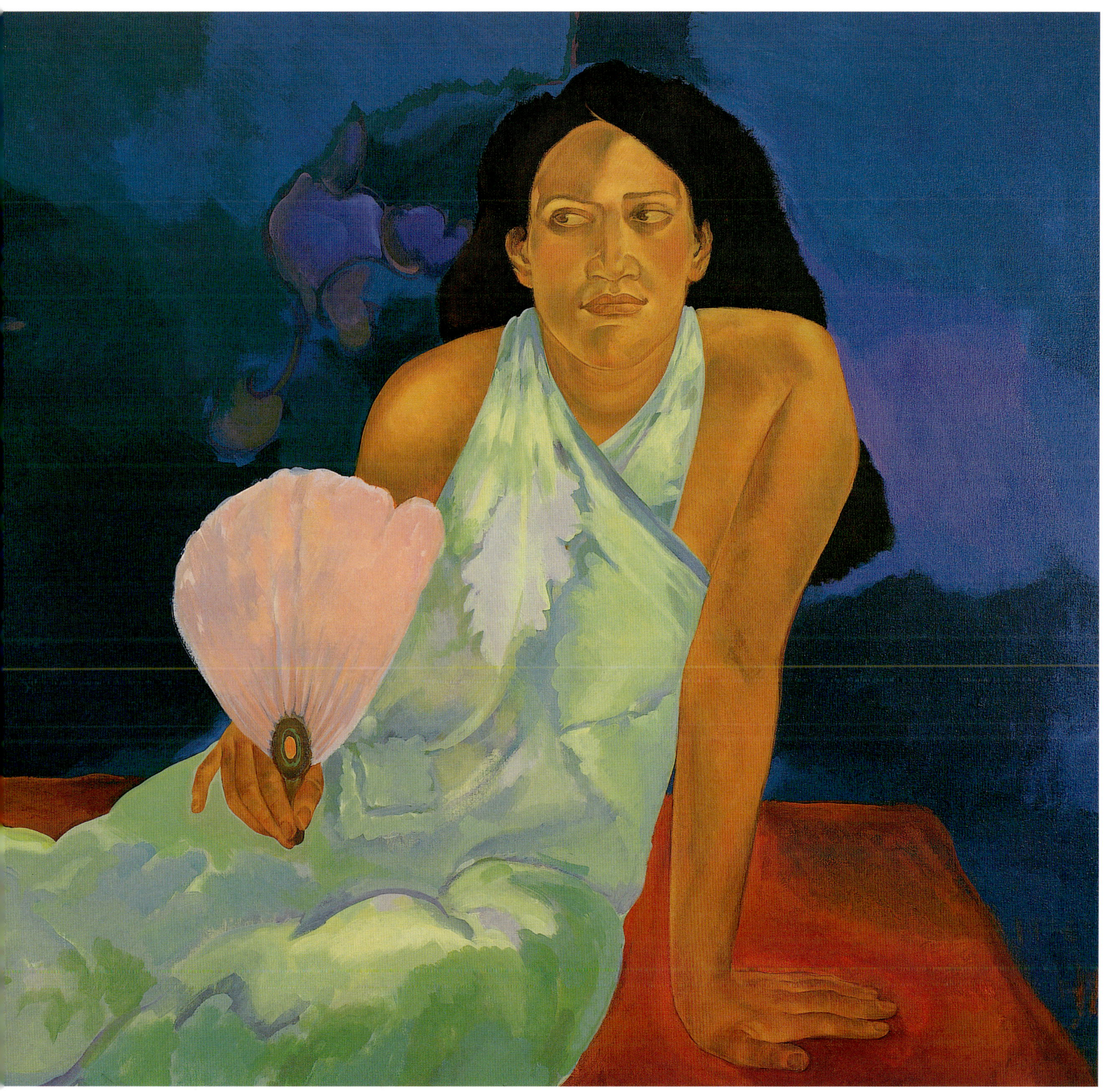

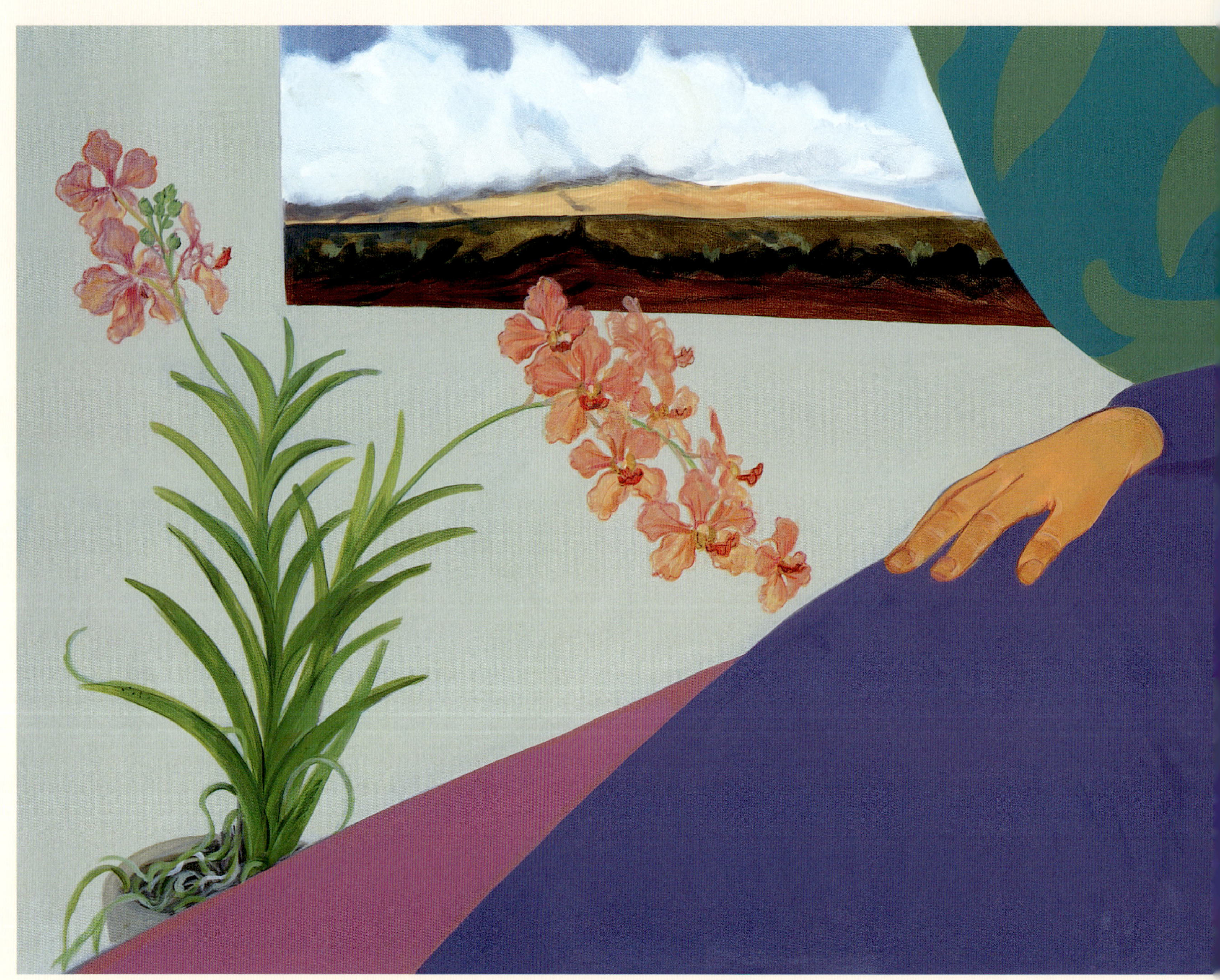

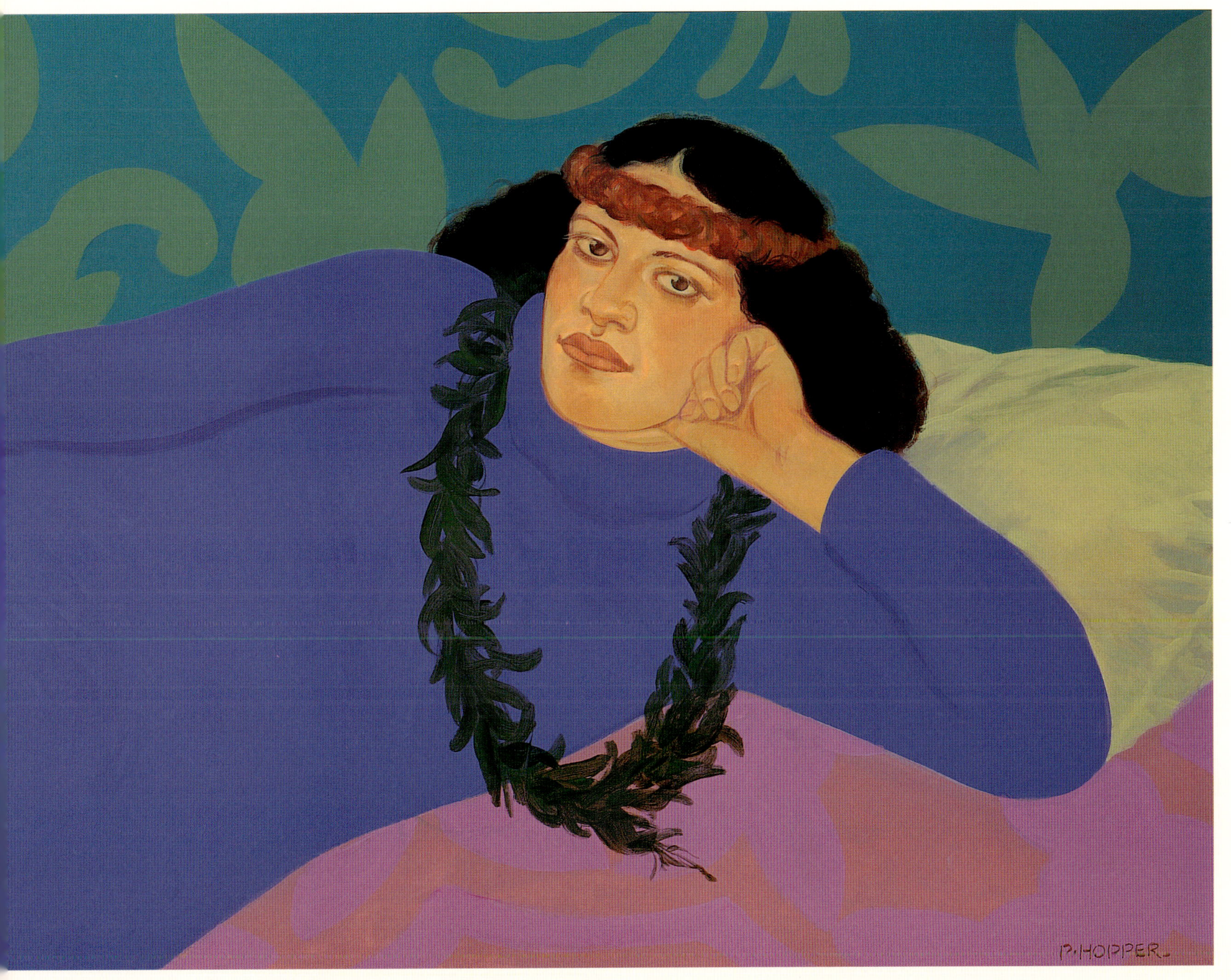
P. HOPPER

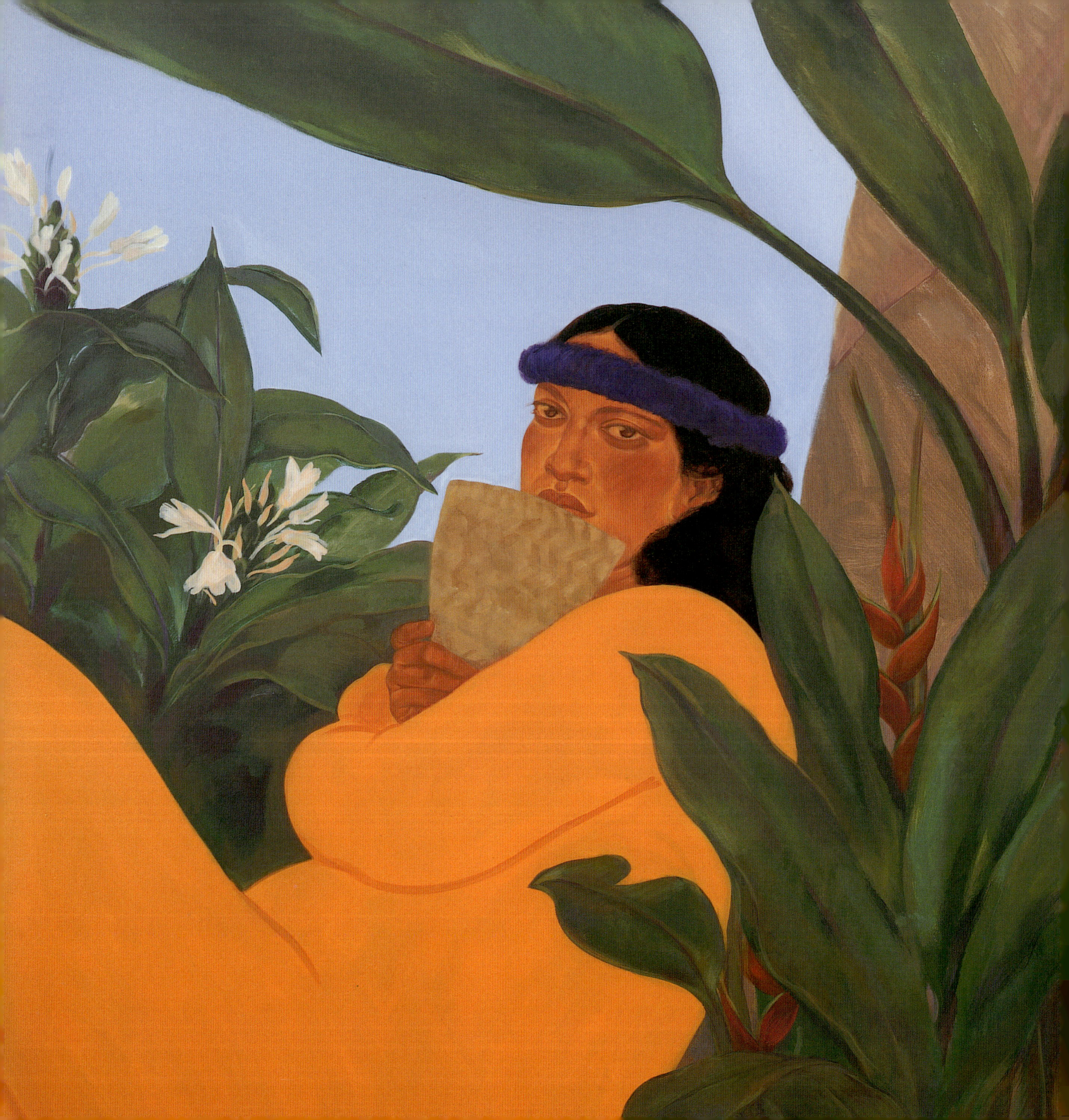

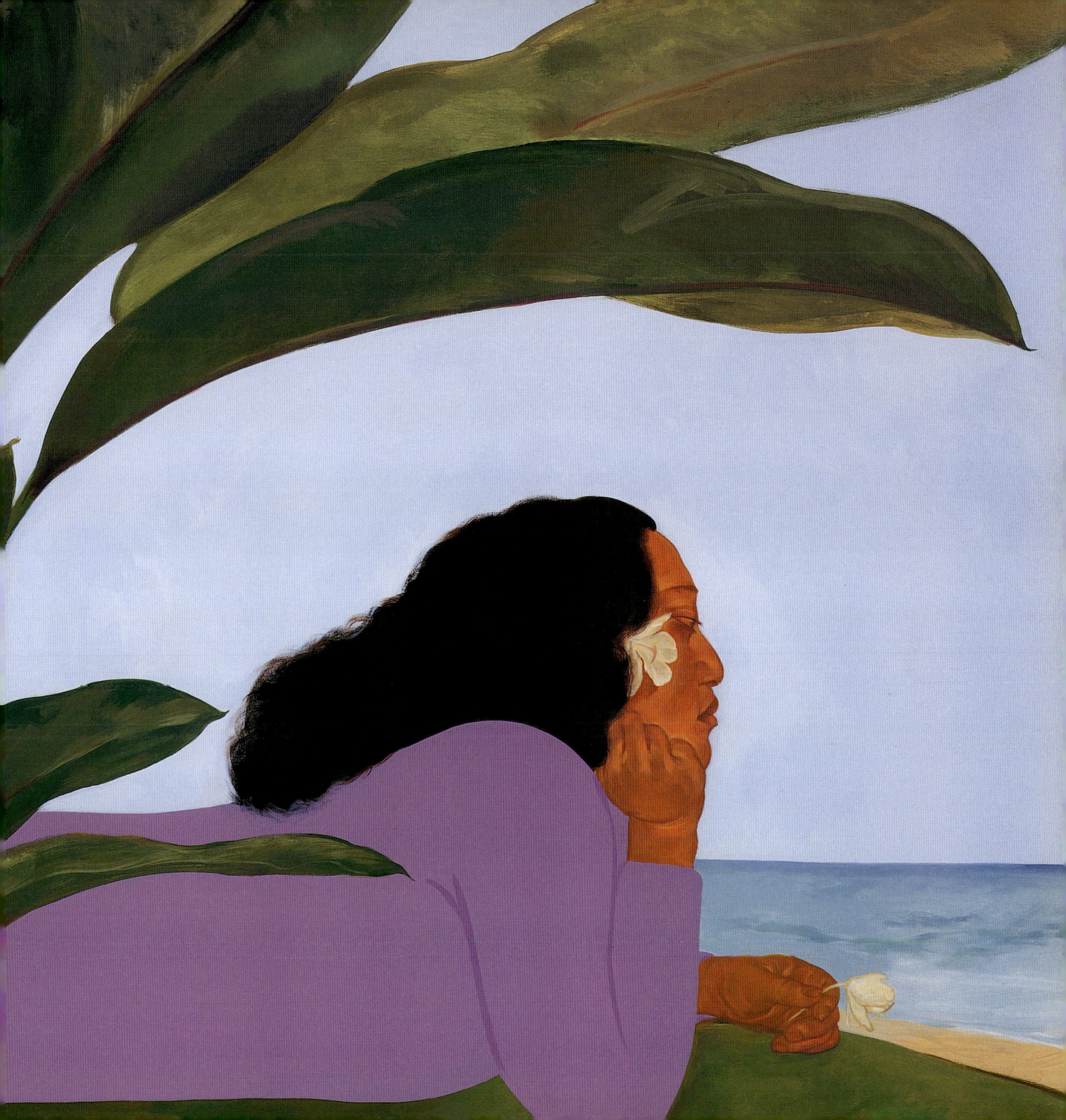

{PREVIOUS} *Walk Across the Sea*
4 x 8 feet, acrylic on canvas, 1999
Private collection (Painted for the 1998 Honolulu telephone book cover)

Hoku (star)
20 x 30 inches, limited edition lithograph, 1990
Private collection

{OPPOSITE} *Mahina* (moon)
20 x 30 inches, limited edition lithograph, 1990
Private collection

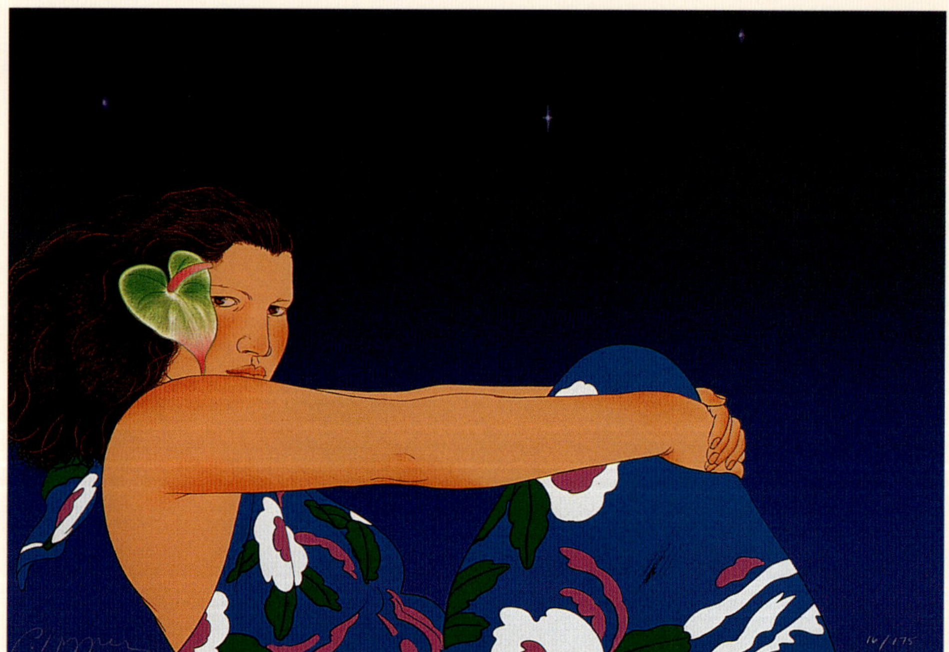

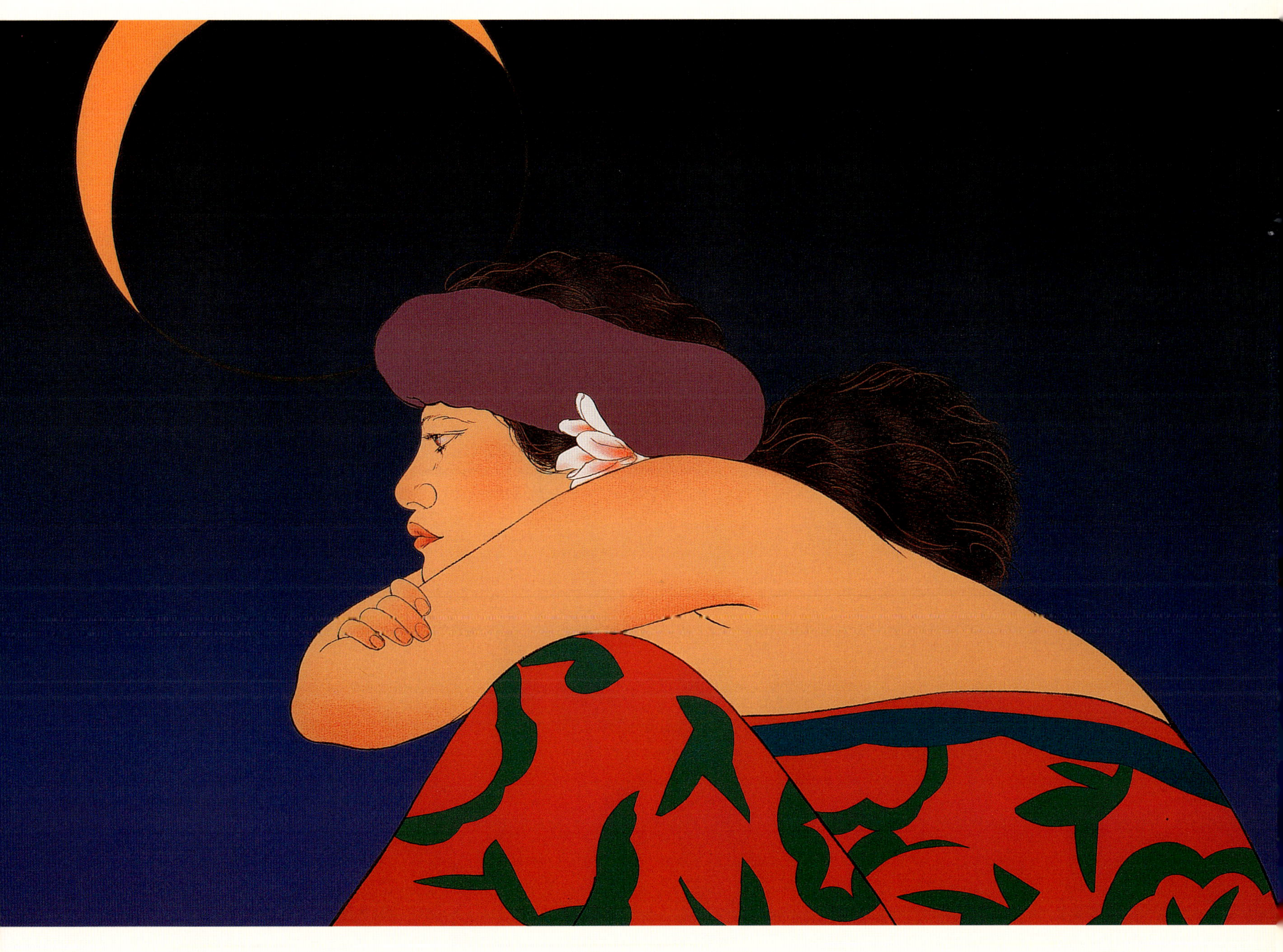

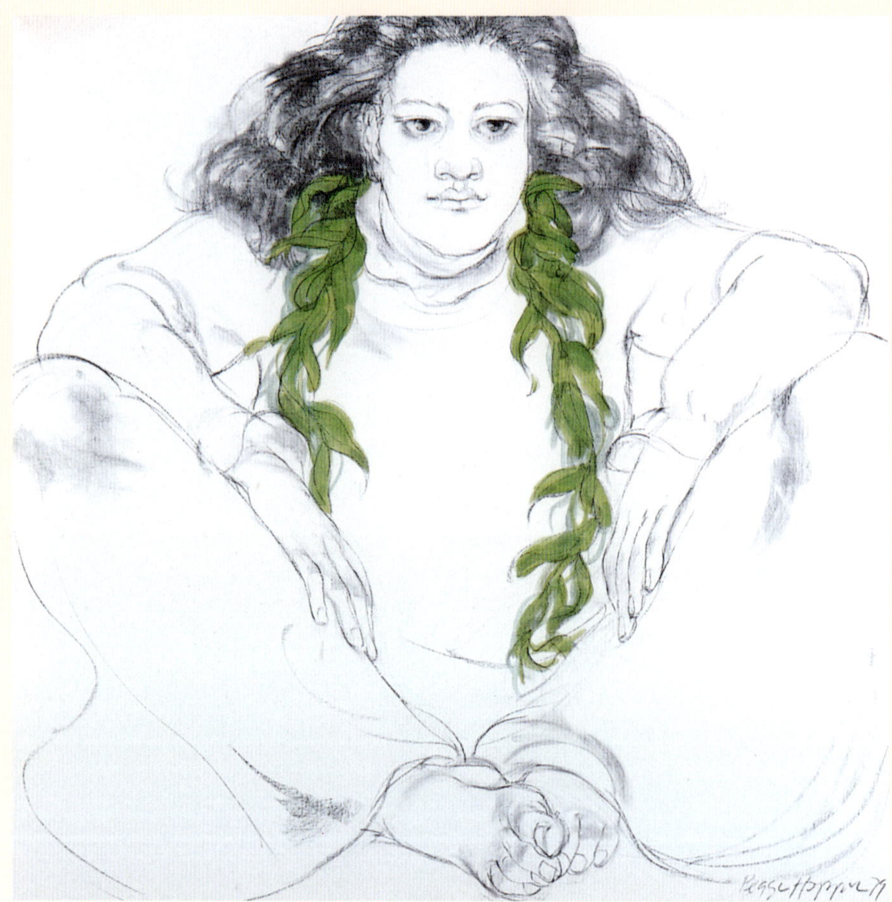

Maile Lei
4 x 4 feet, charcoal and acrylic
on canvas, 1979
Collection of the artist

{OPPOSITE} *Pink Lei*
3 x 3 feet, charcoal and acrylic
on canvas, 1979
Collection of the artist

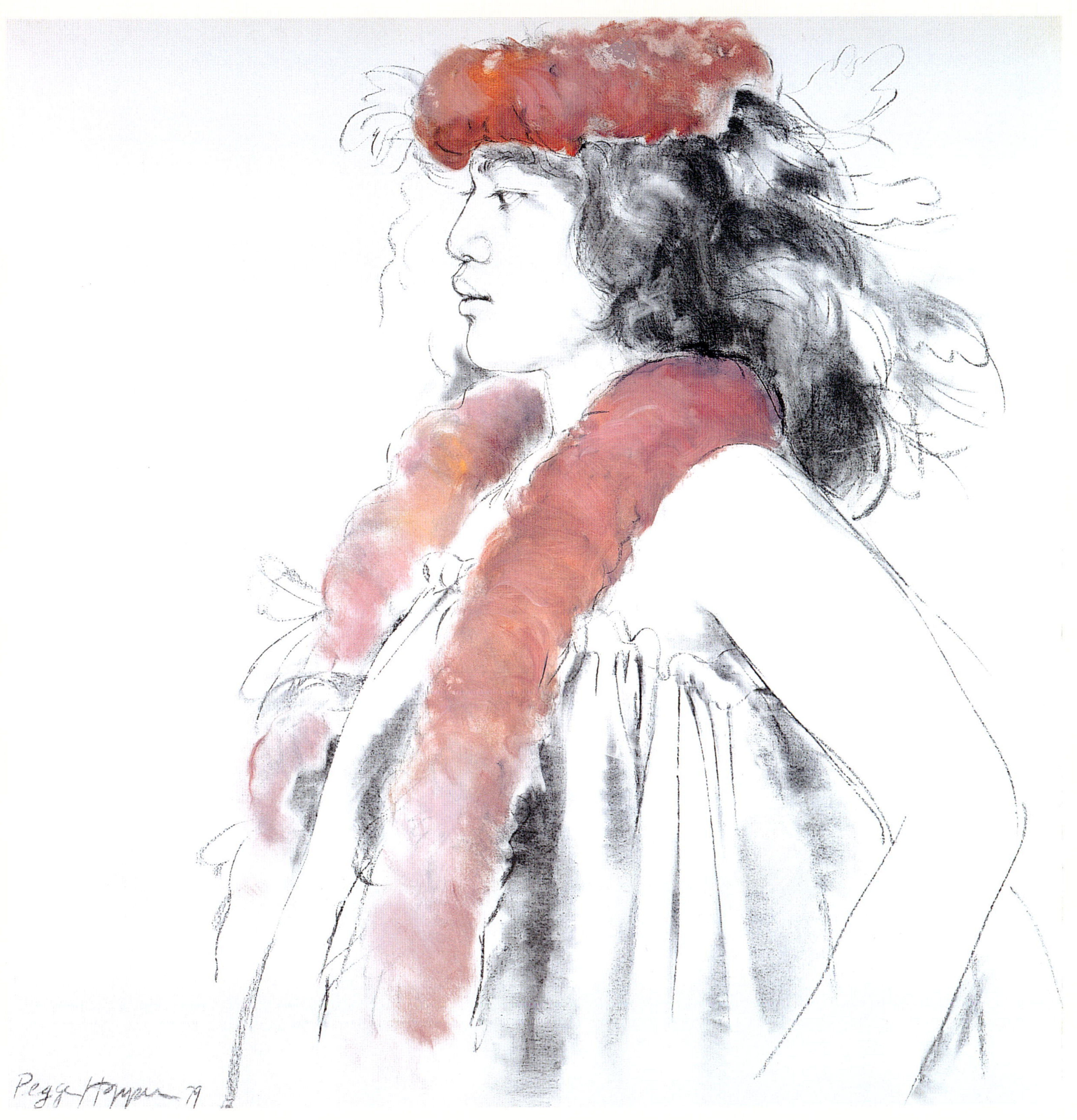
Pegge Hopper 79

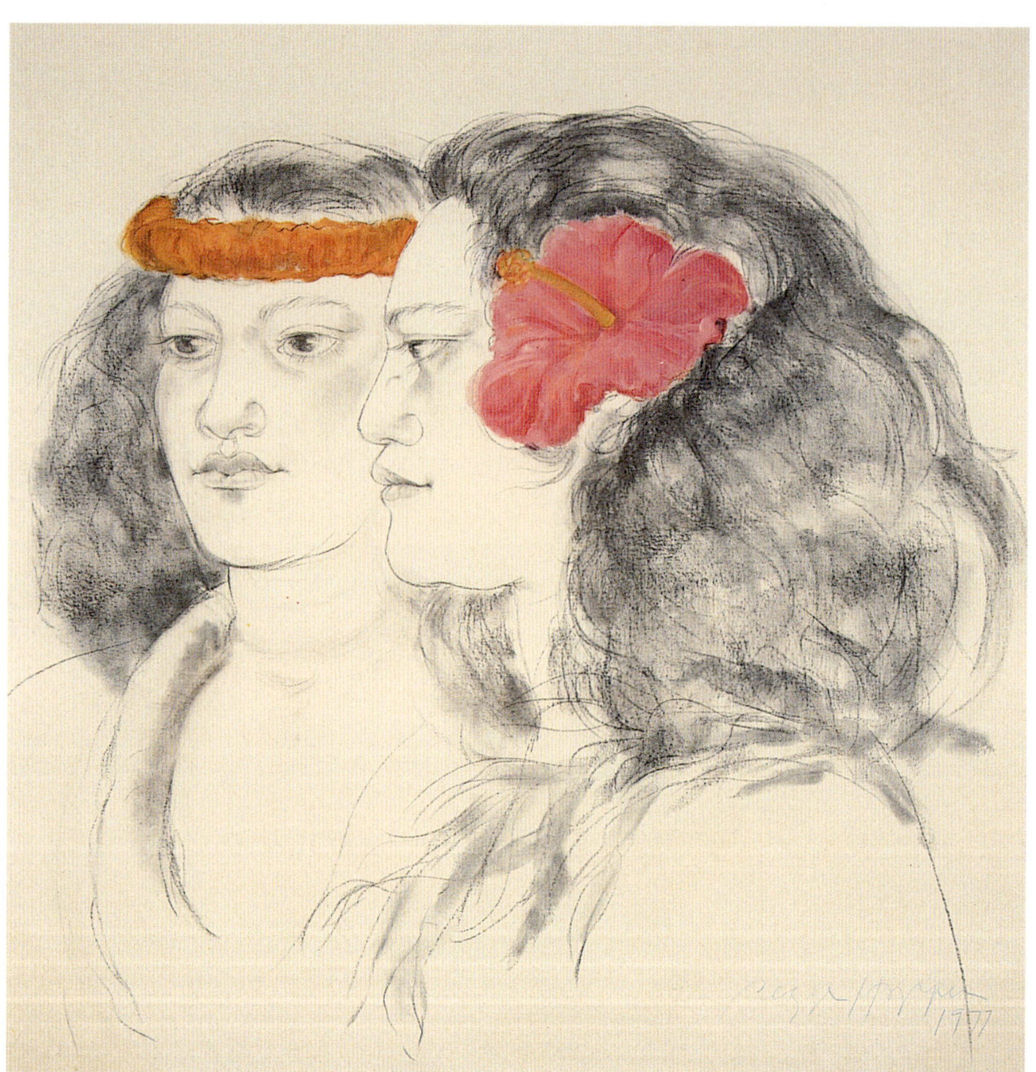

Untitled
40 x 40 inches, charcoal and acrylic on canvas, circa 1979
Private collection

{OPPOSITE} *Untitled*
20 x 14 inches, pastel on paper, circa 1979
Private collection

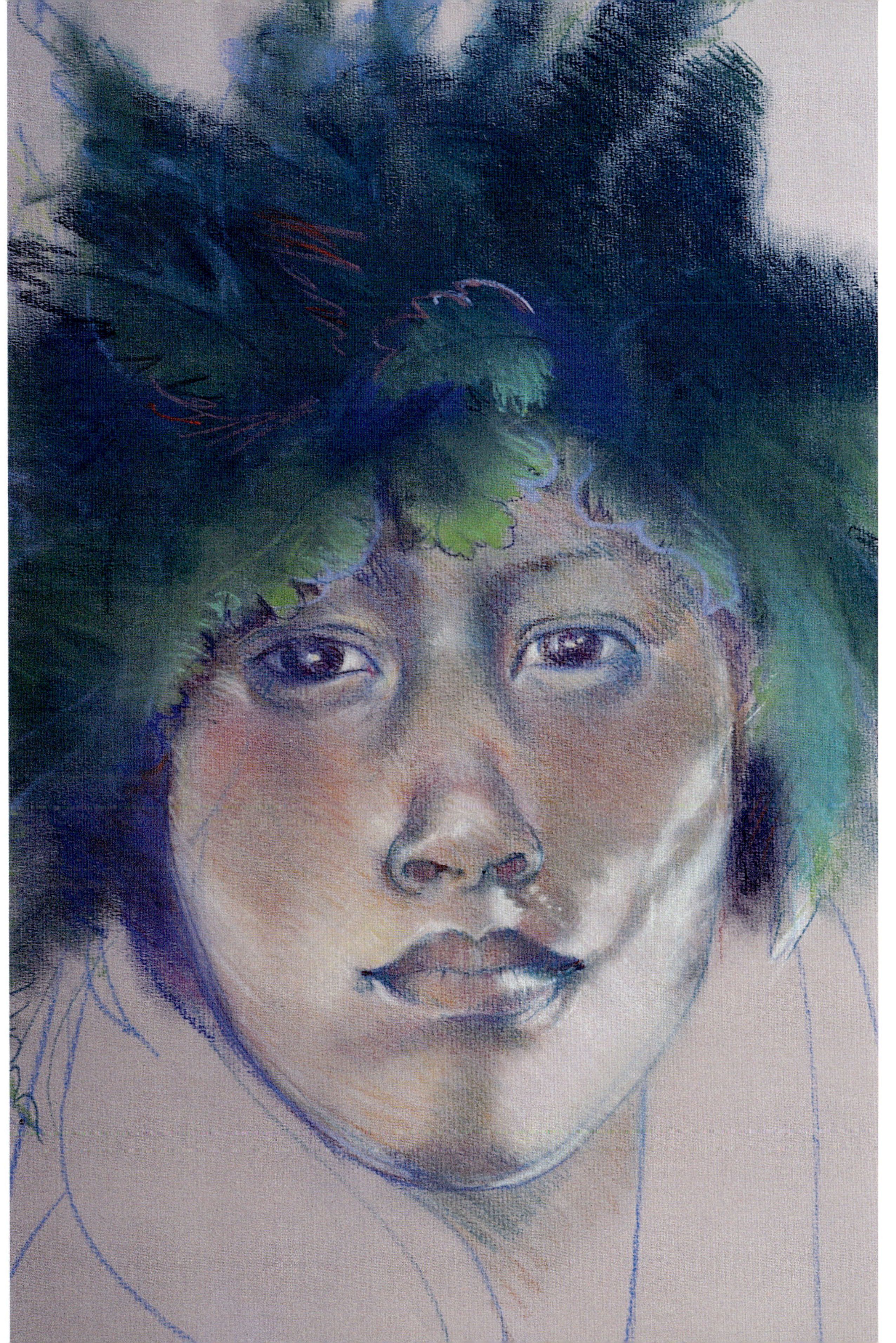

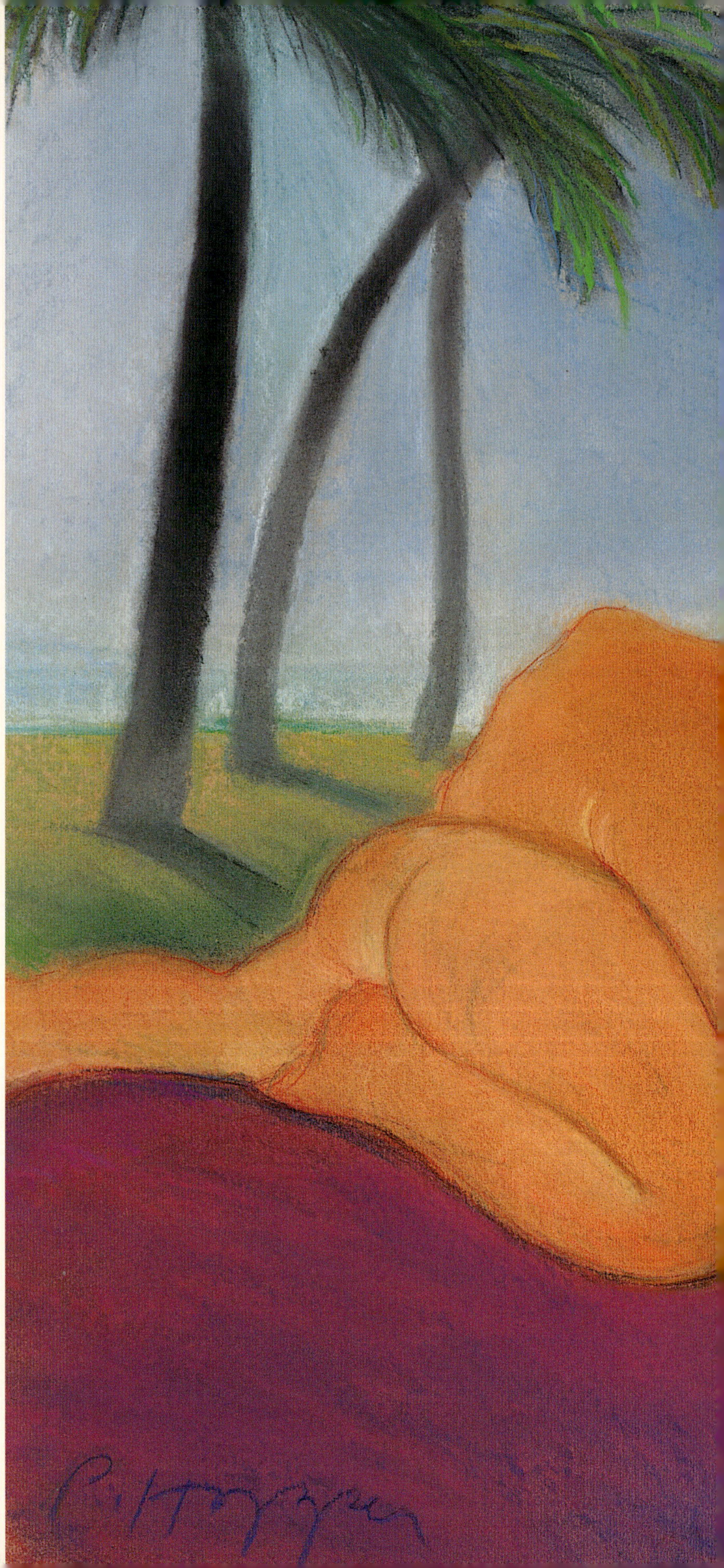

Nurturing Life with Love
16 x 24 inches, pastel on paper, 1989
Private collection (Created for the Healthy Mothers, Healthy Babies organization)

{BELOW} *Precious Gift*
16 x 24 inches, pastel on paper, 1987
Collection of the artist (Created for the Mother's Milk Bank)

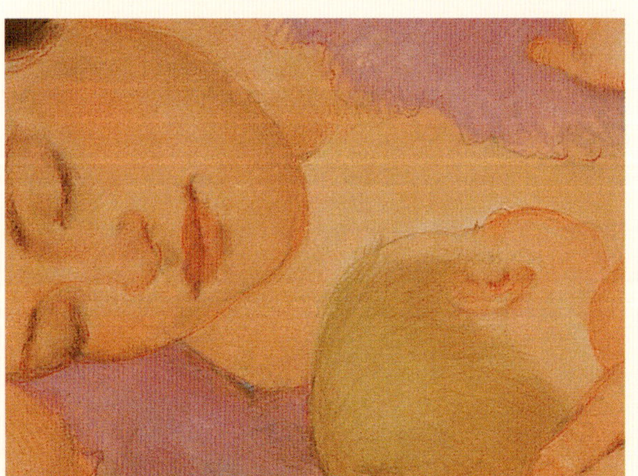

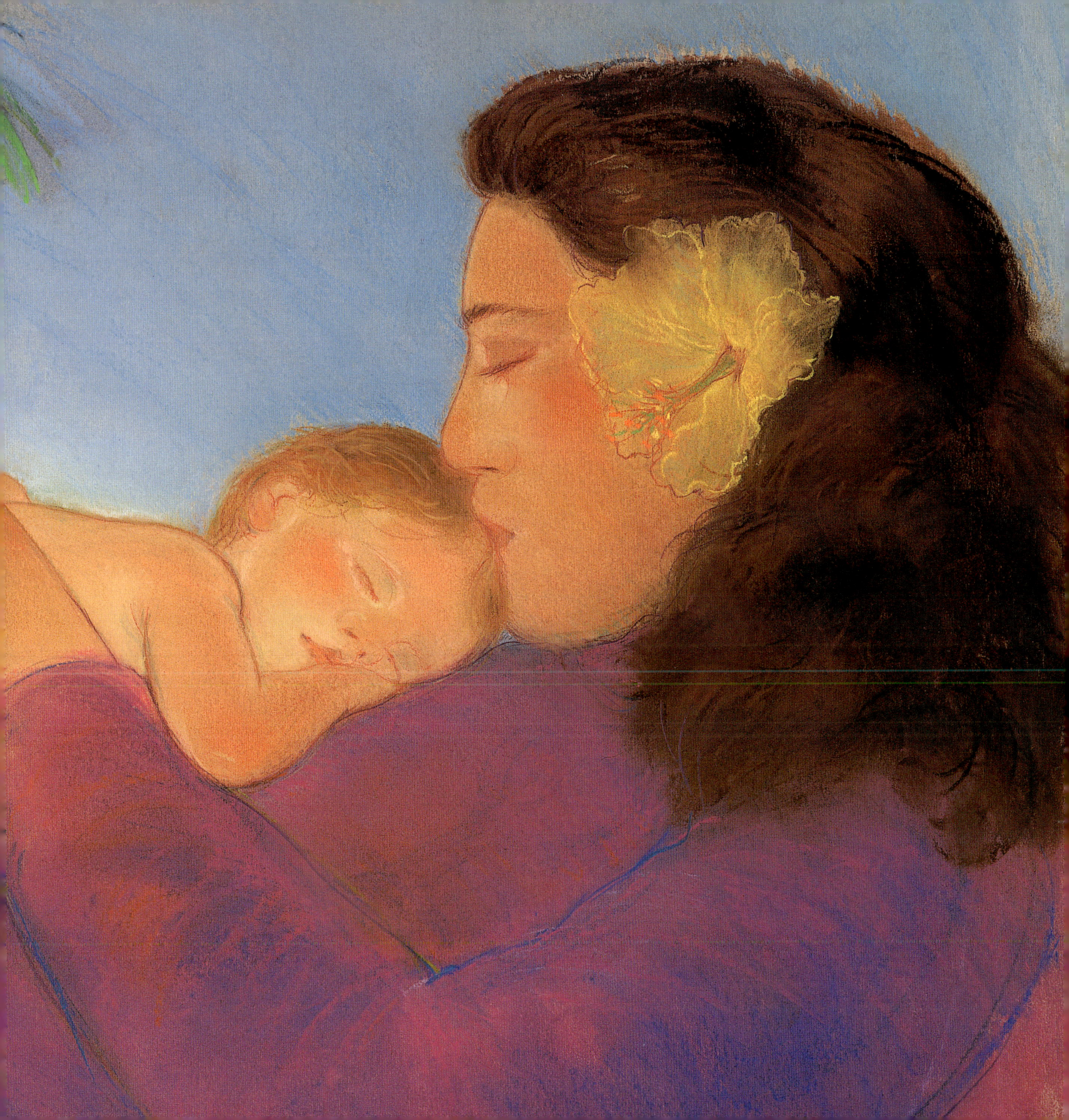

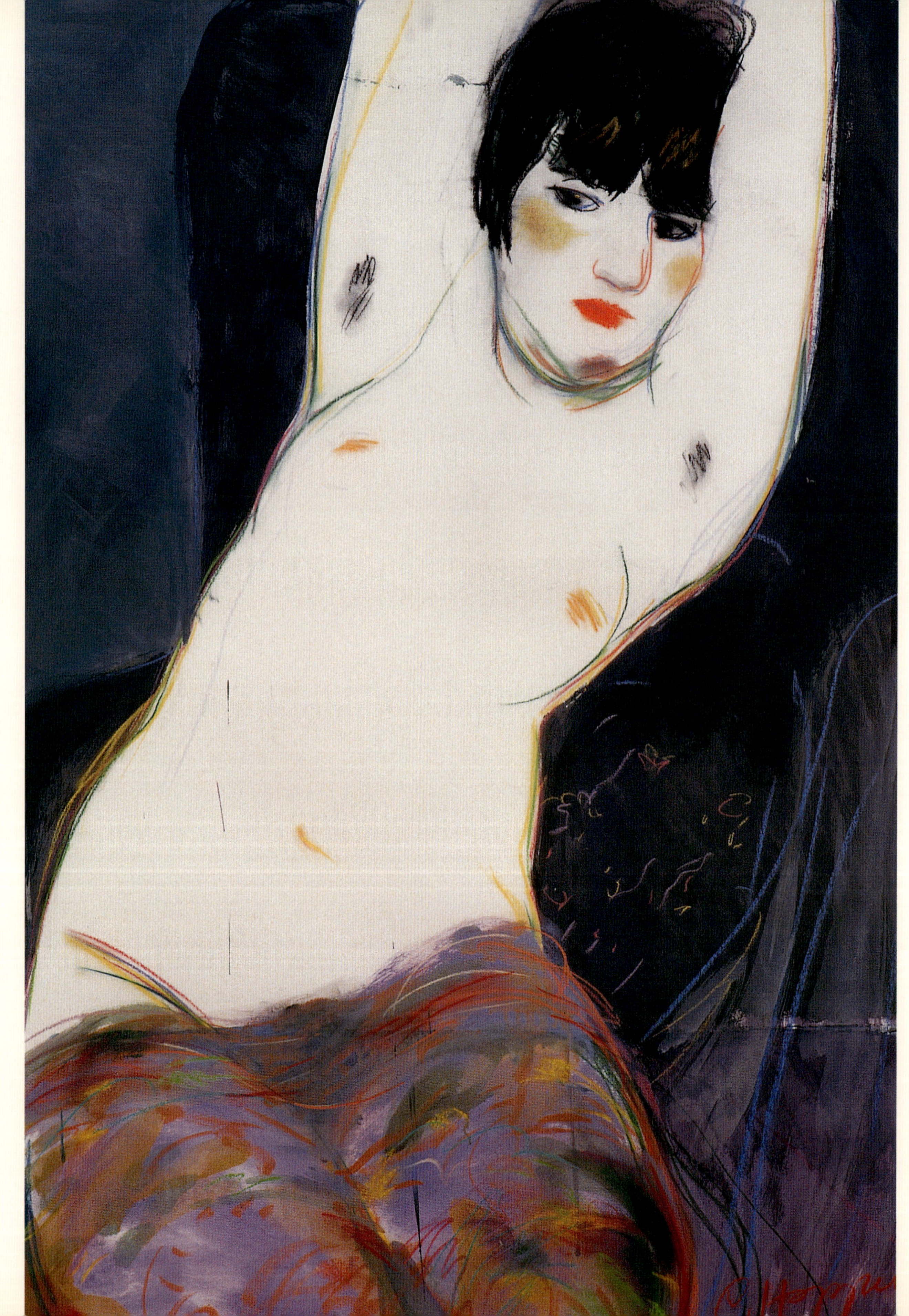

Kiki
44 x 30 inches, acrylic and pastel on paper, 1986
Pegge Hopper Gallery, Honolulu

Untitled
3 x 2 feet, mixed media on paper, 1989
Collection of the artist

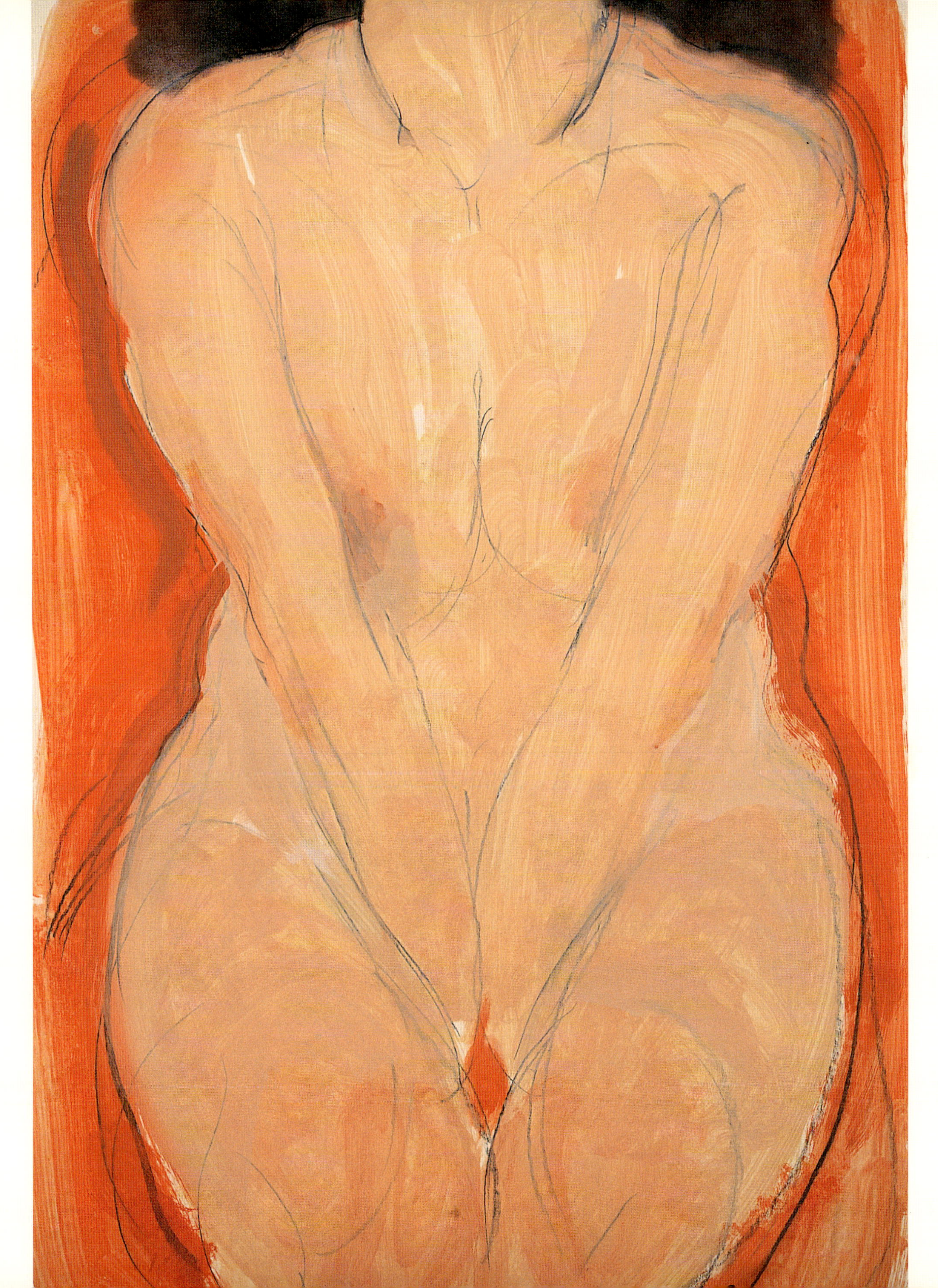

Untitled Sketch
24 x 18 inches, conté on paper, 1991
Collection of the artist

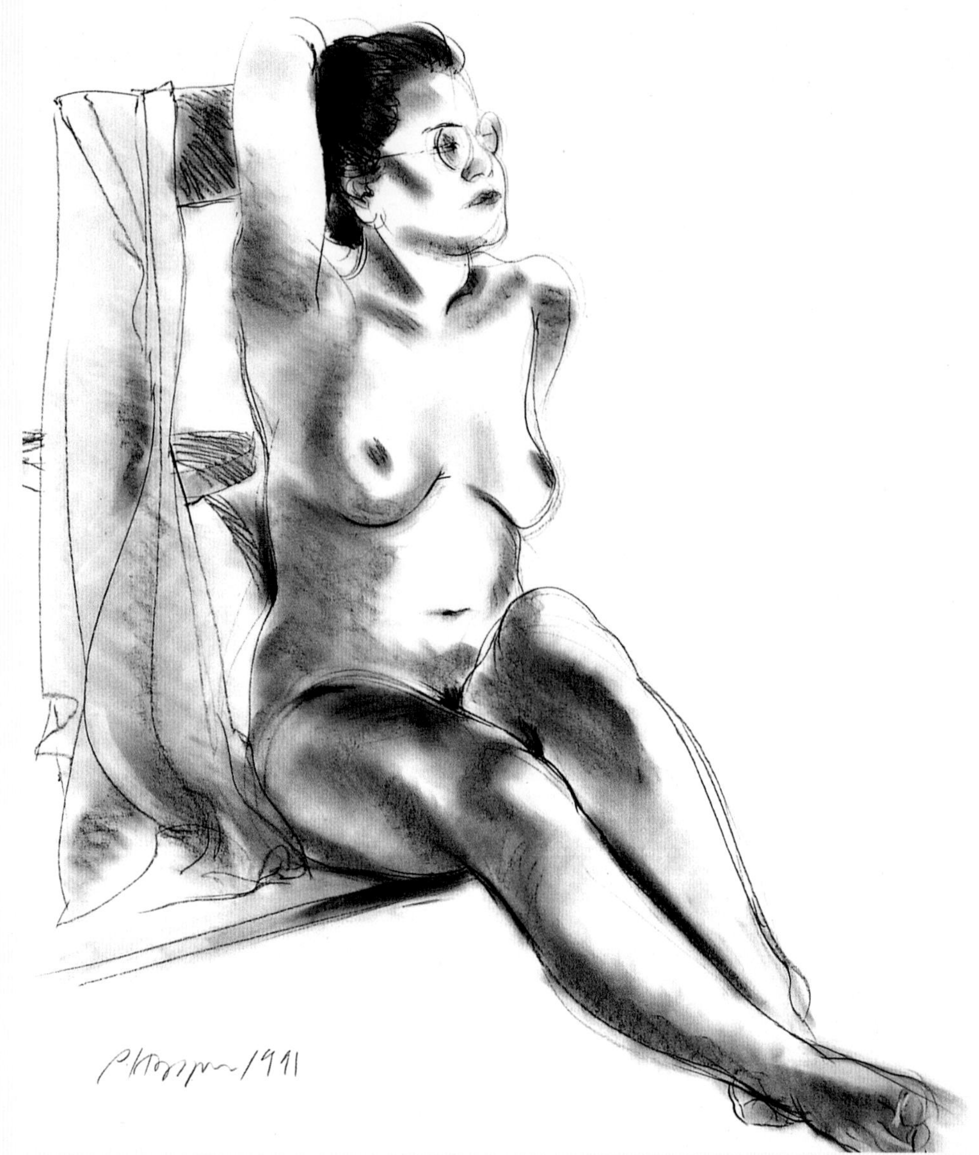

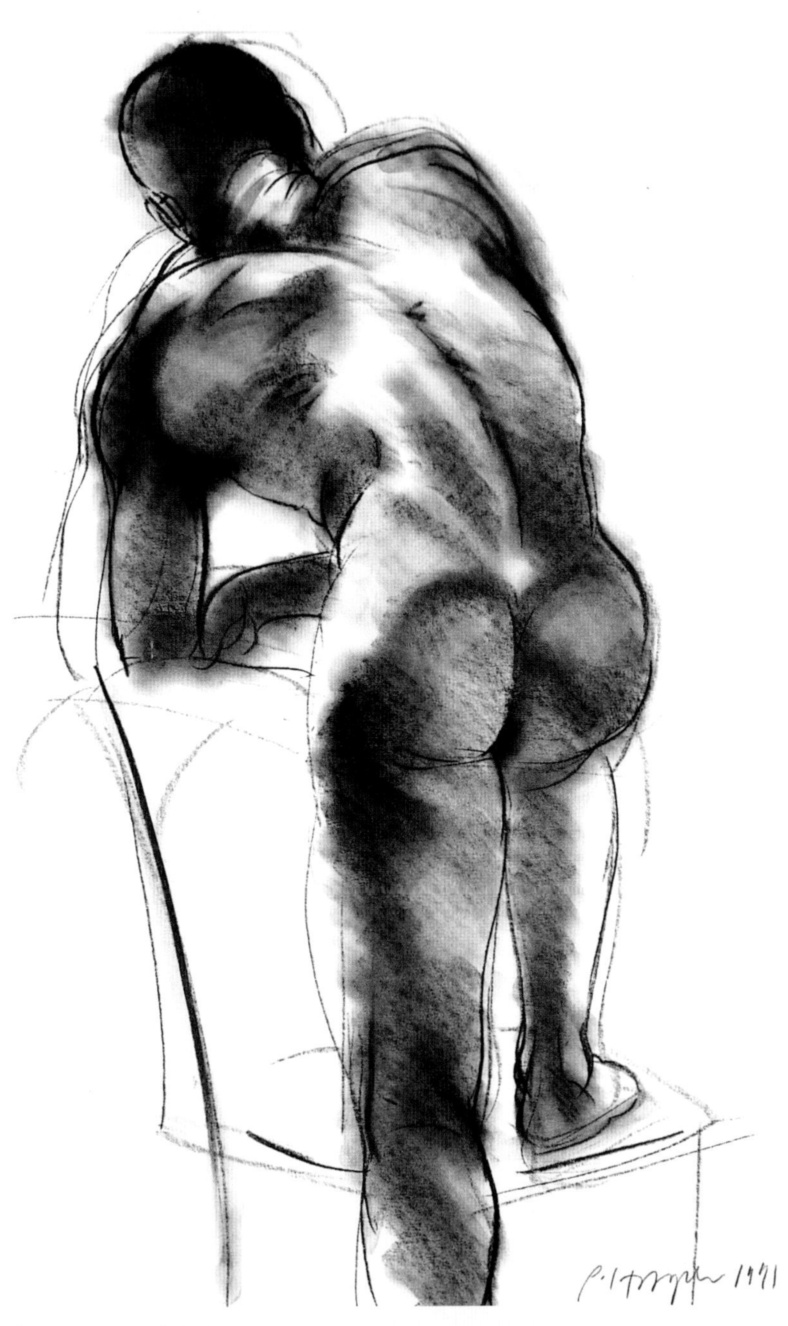

Untitled Sketch
24 x 20 inches, conté on paper, 1991
Collection of the artist

Lauren
4 x 6 feet, mixed media on paper, 1989
Private collection

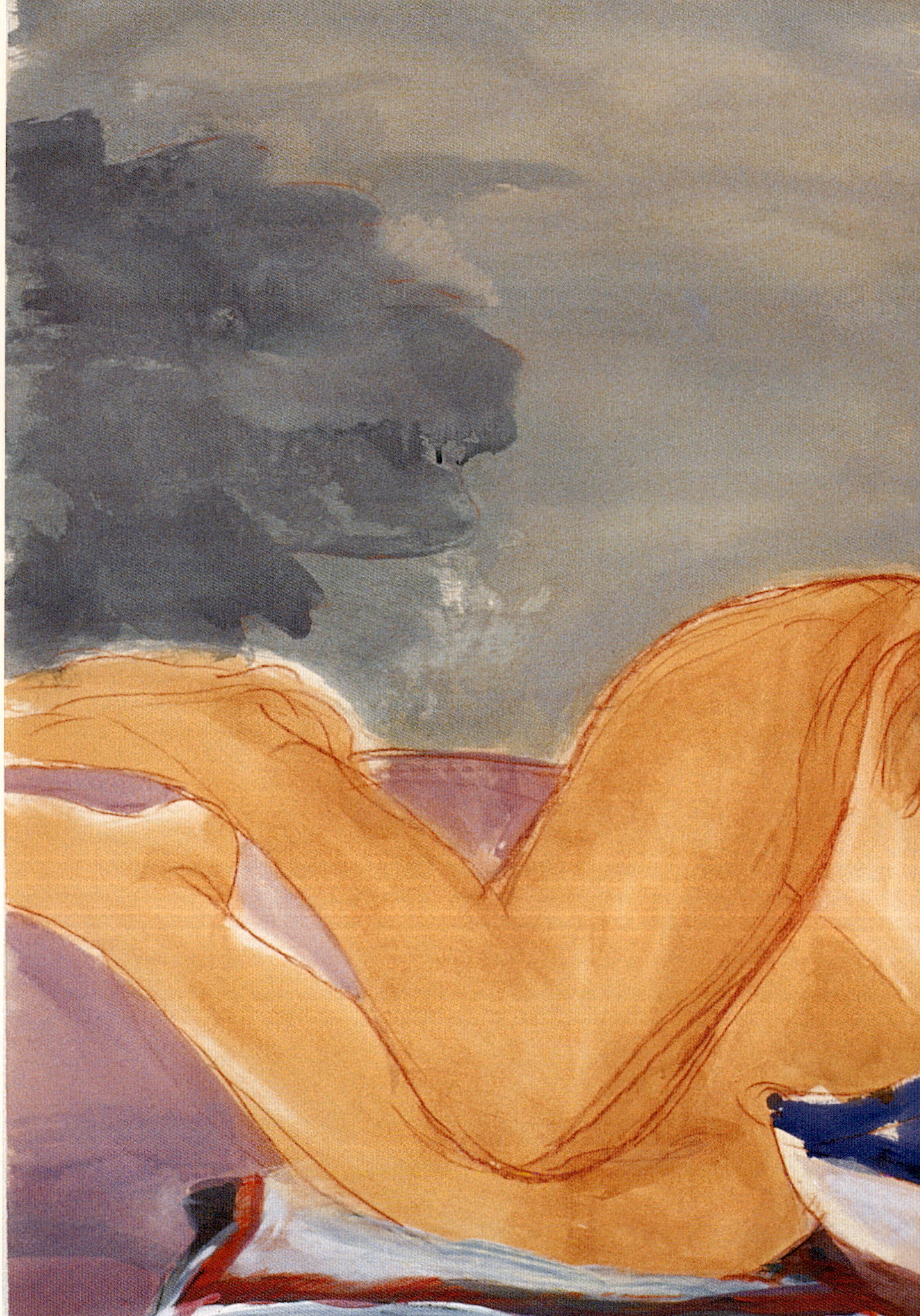

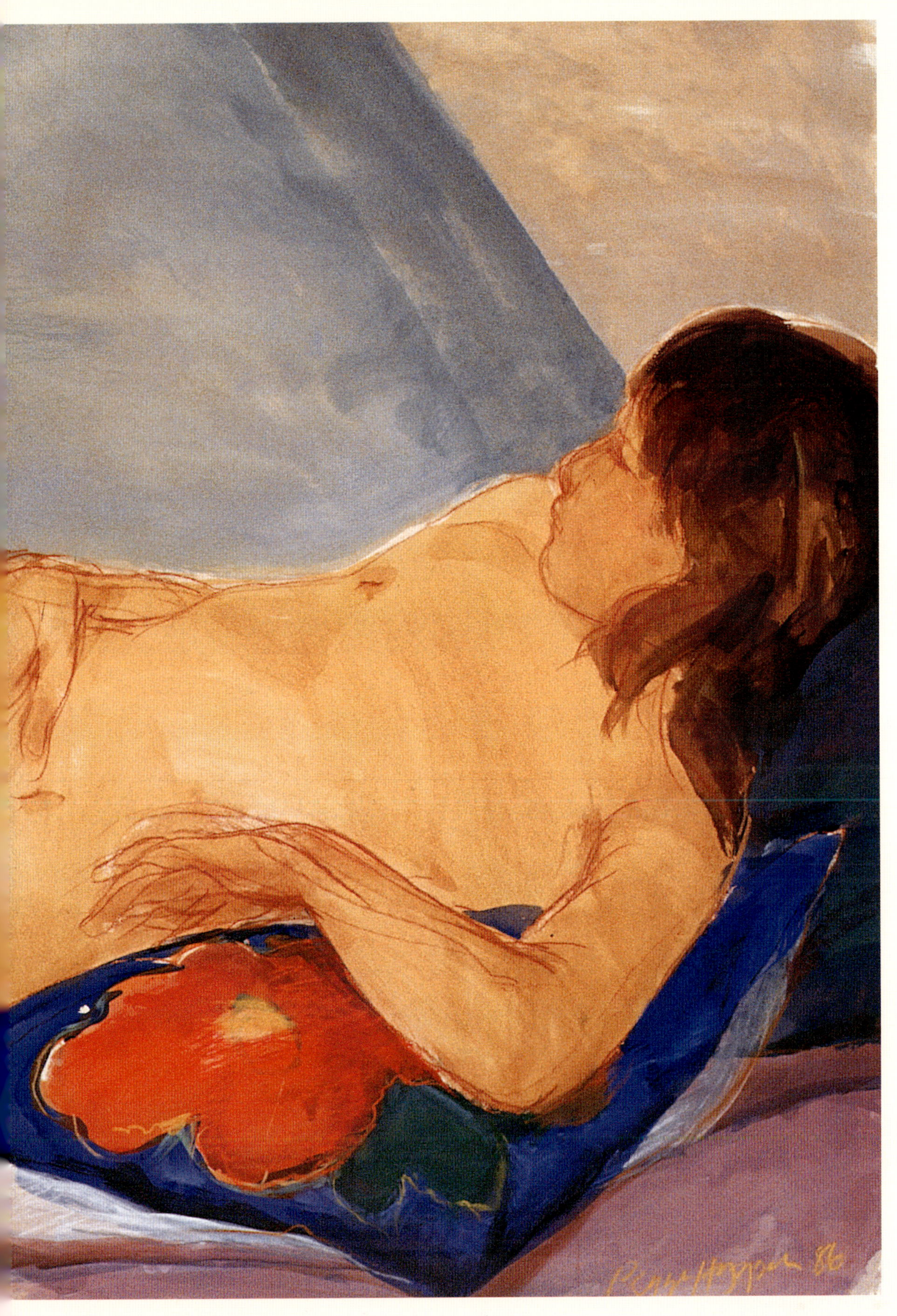

MEXICO

In my second year at Art Center, I read about the Instituto Allende in San Miguel de Allende. I begged my father to allow me to attend. He refused, saying I would just marry a Mexican man and he'd never see me again. It was probably a good thing I remained at Art Center. I received an excellent education there.

In 1979 I saw San Miguel de Allende for the first time when my husband and I took our two oldest daughters to Mexico. I returned to San Miguel in 1989 and was determined to build a house, which I did from 1990 to 1996. The experience was wonderful and because of it I've gained a real love for architecture and a great respect for the discipline.

Calavera
14 x 12 inches, pastel on paper, 1991
Collection of the artist

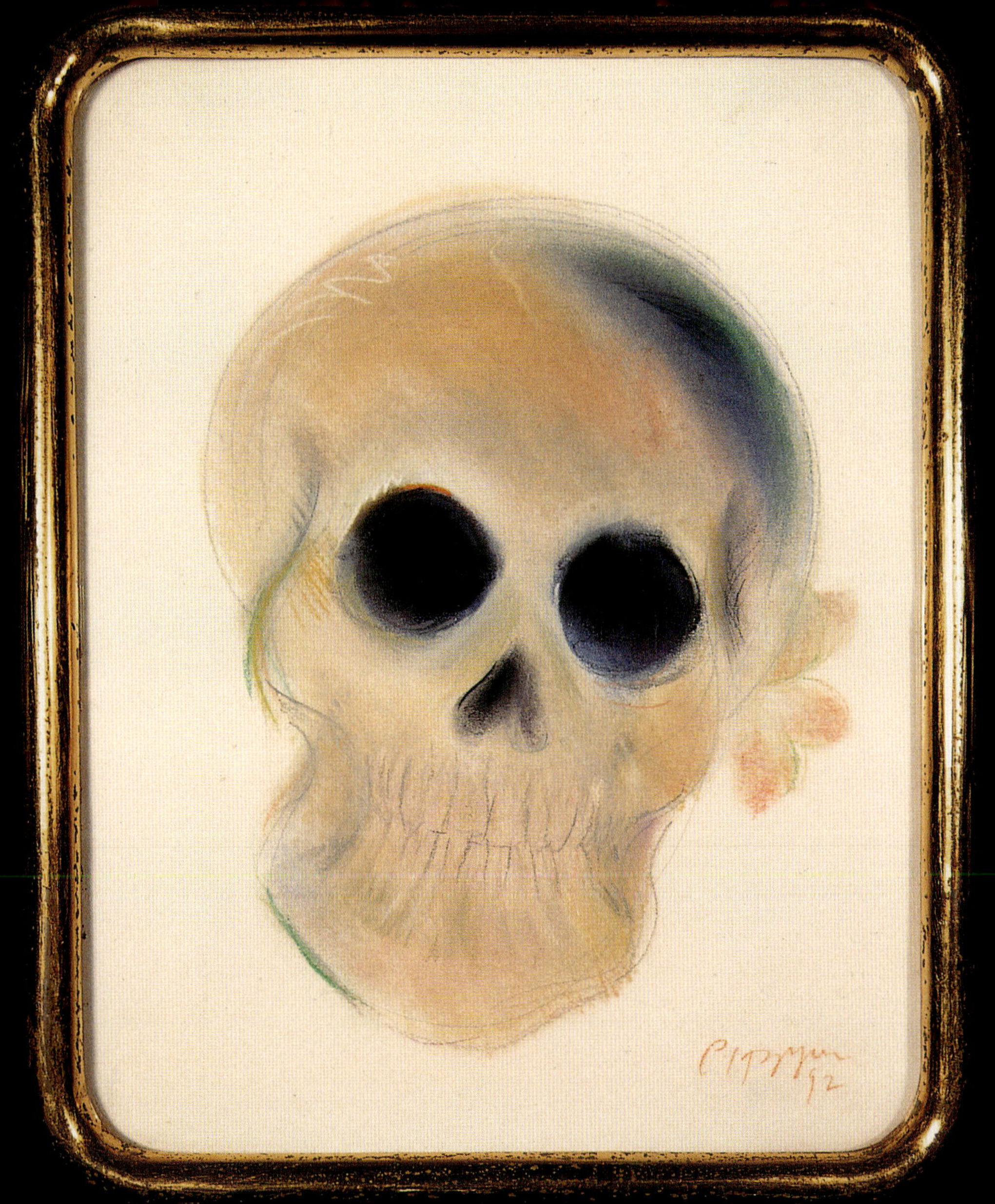

Day of the Dead

6 x 4 feet, mixed media on paper, 1994

Collection of the artist

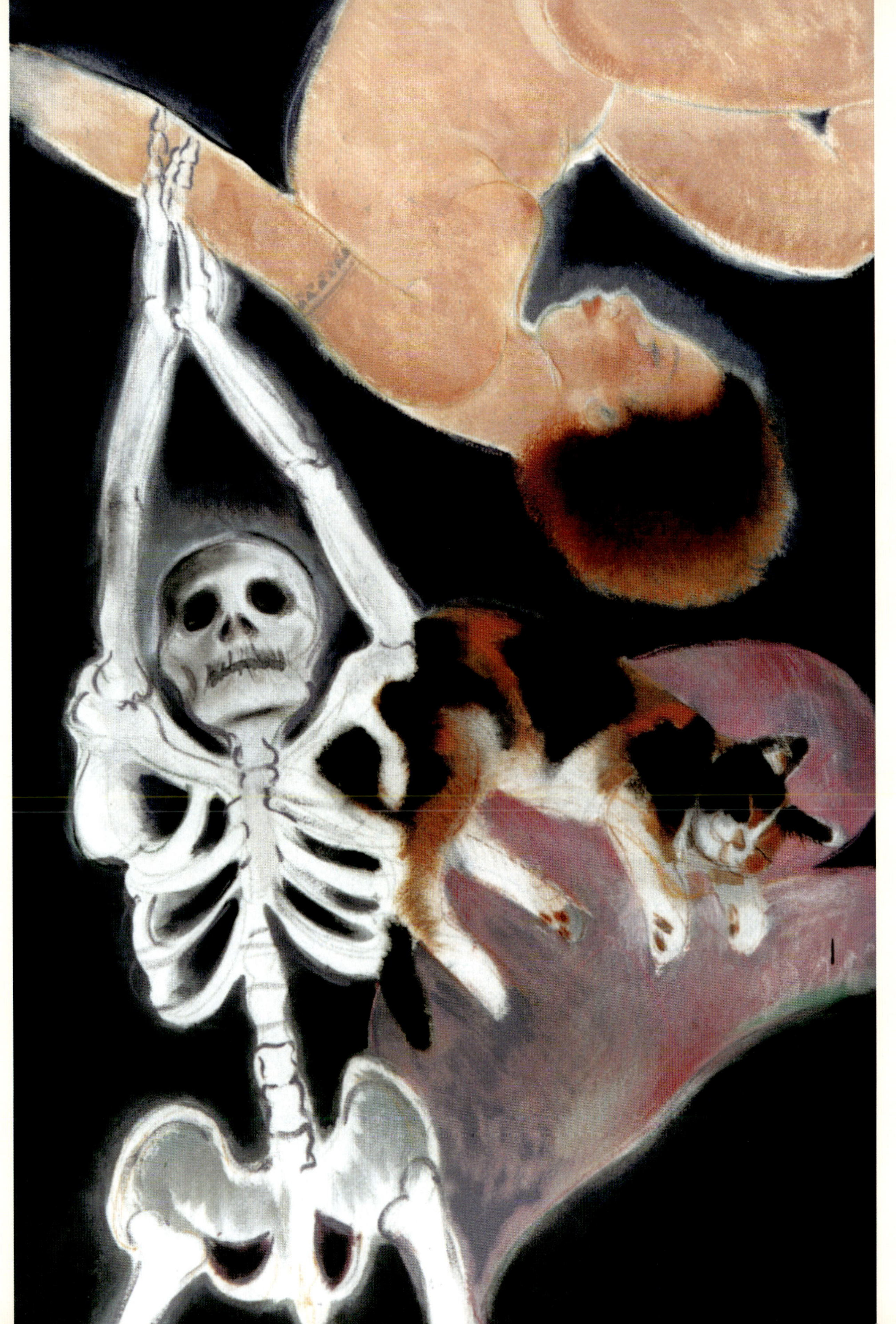

Promotional Poster
16 x 24 inches, offset lithography,
circa 1994
International Film Festival, Honolulu

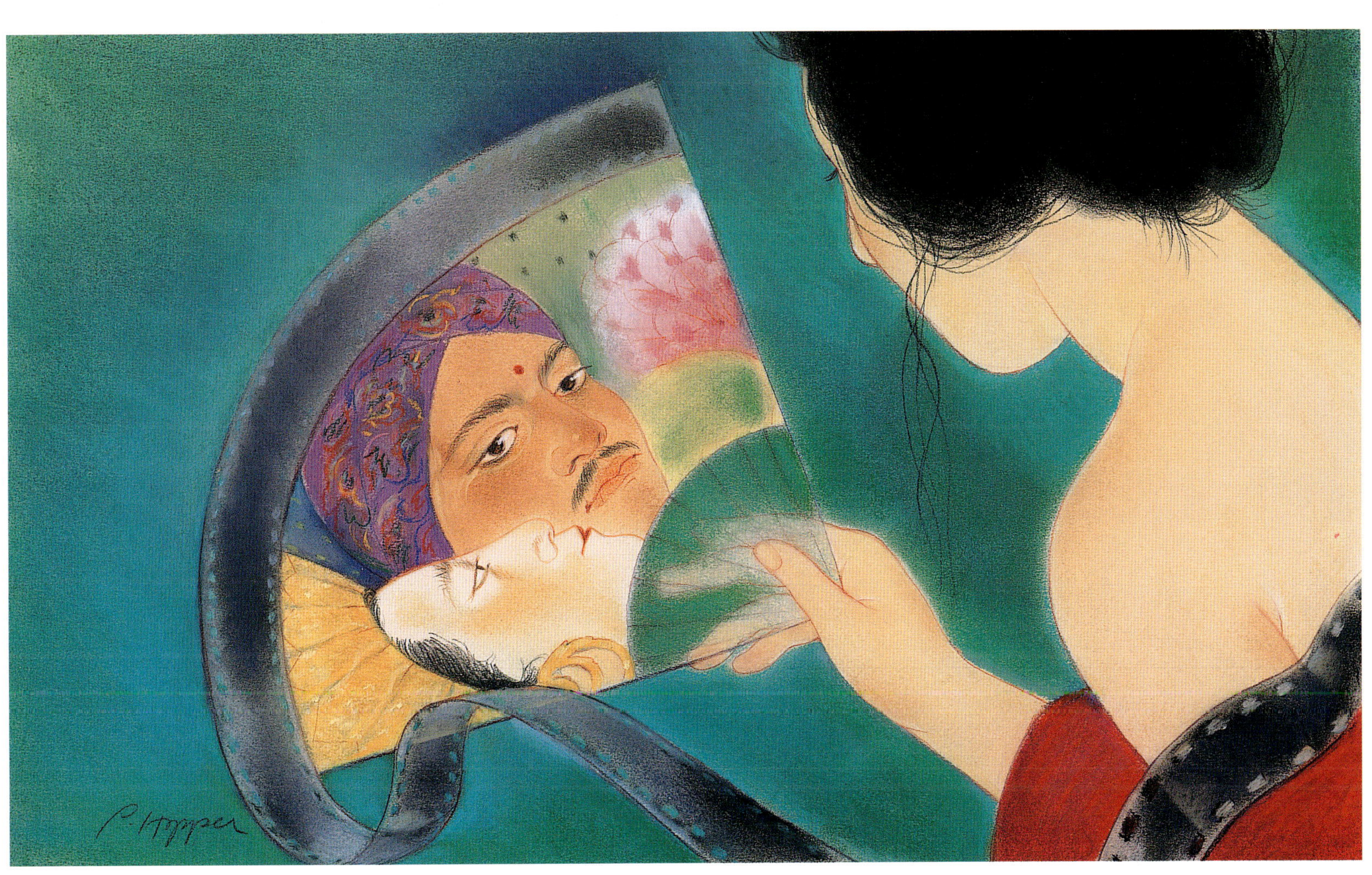

CERAMIC SLIPPERS

I took a ceramics class at the Honolulu Academy of Arts and started making these ceramic slippers. The rubber slipper—ubiquitous in Hawai`i—is the universal footwear, so perfectly designed. The shape inspired me to have some fun.

painted clay, 1992
Private collections

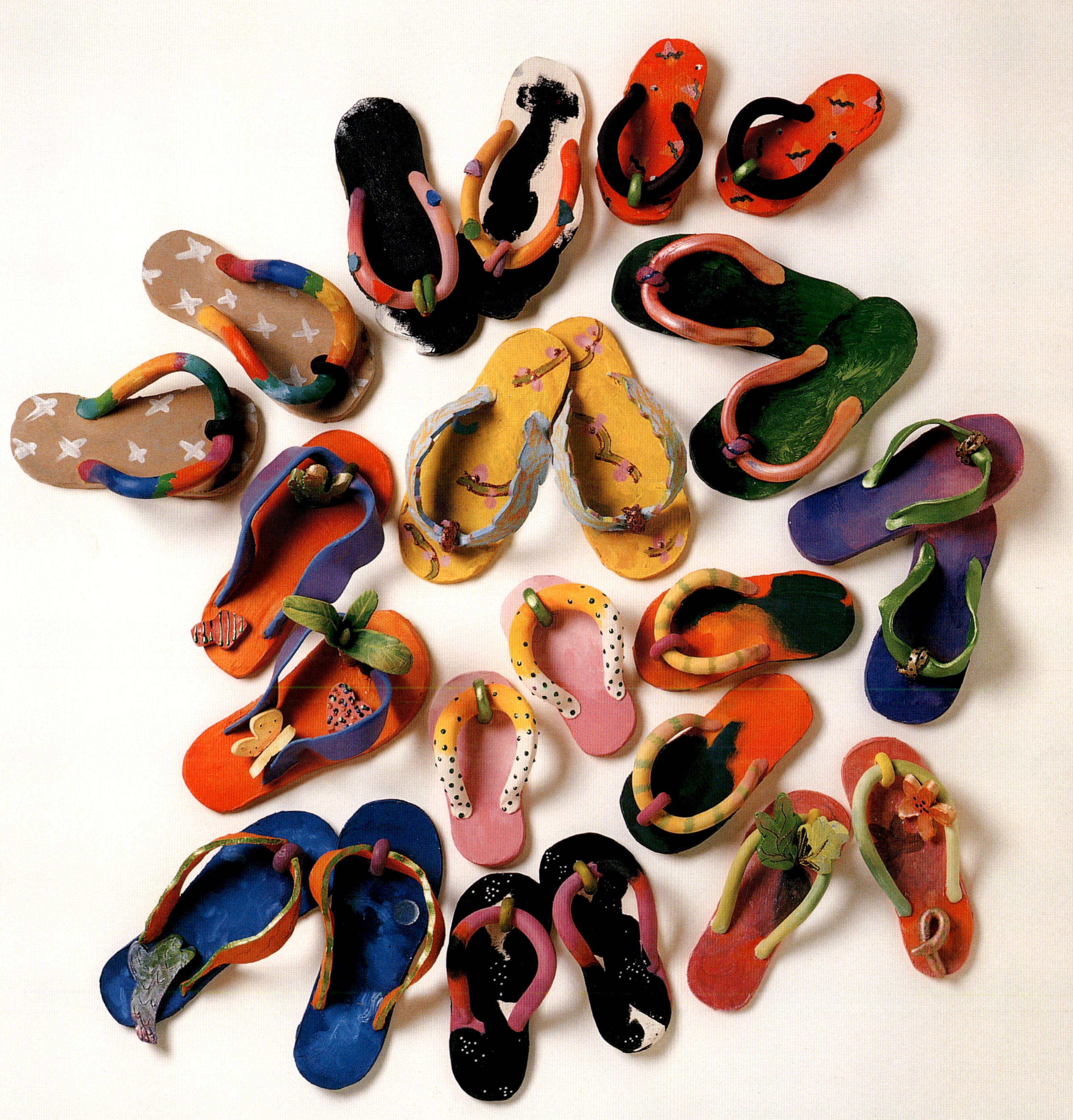

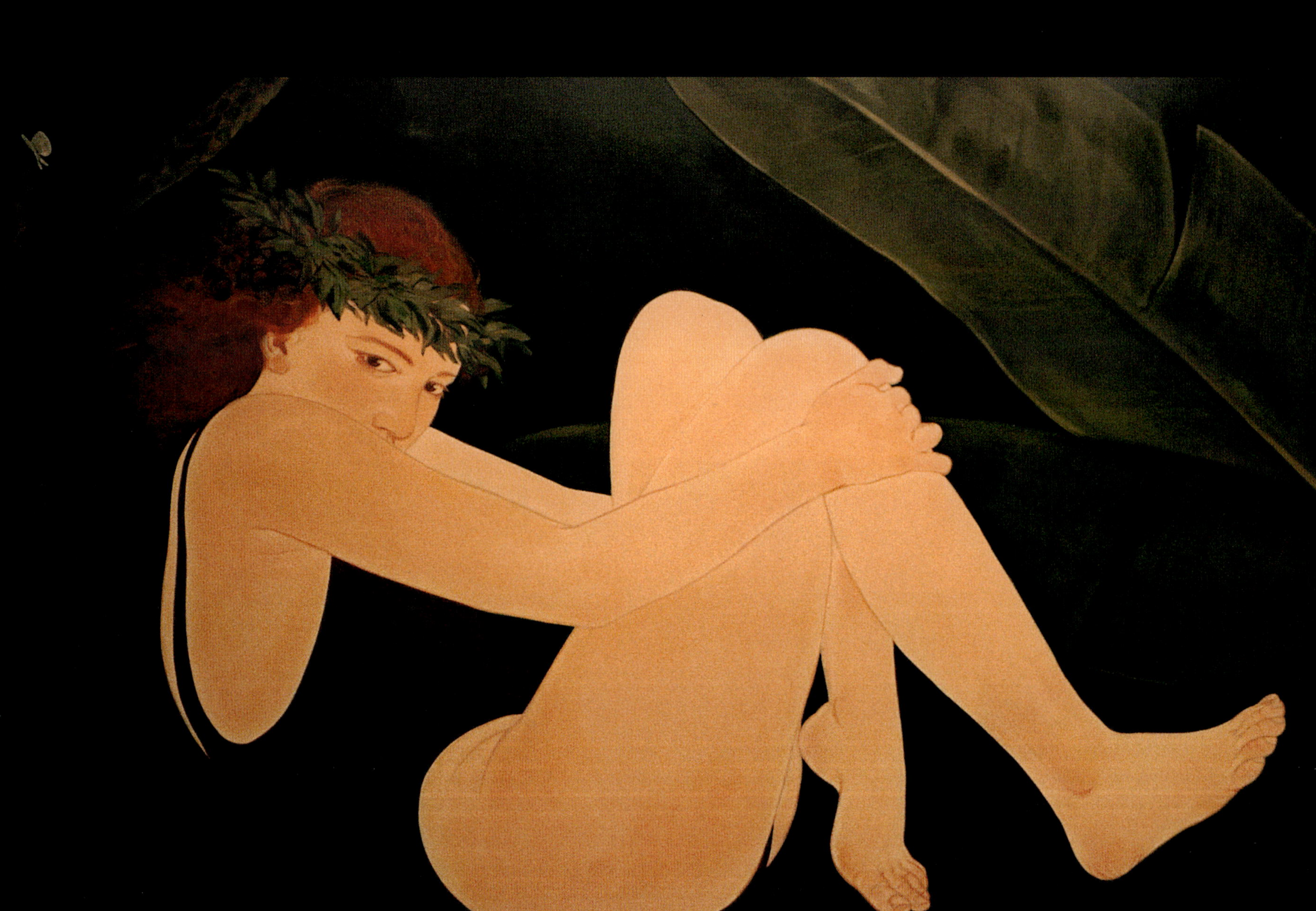

Lauren, the Lady in the Moon
4 x 6 feet, acrylic on canvas, 1993
Private collection

FAREWELL ALOHA

Aloha, Aloha was painted in protest against and in commemoration of the cruel murder of a young woman in Honolulu. The broken lei is composed of skulls, the face of the woman that was killed, and the faces of the three other young female murder victims whose cases went unsolved. For me this was the end of an age of innocence. No longer did I leave my doors unlocked or let my daughters run free.

Aloha, Aloha
5 x 4 feet, acrylic on canvas, 1978
Collection of the artist

{OVERLEAF} *Lahainaluna*
4 x 3 feet, oil on canvas, 1981
Collection of the artist (Created for a poster commemorating the 150th anniversary of the Lahainaluna school in Maui, one of the oldest public schools west of the Rocky Mountains)

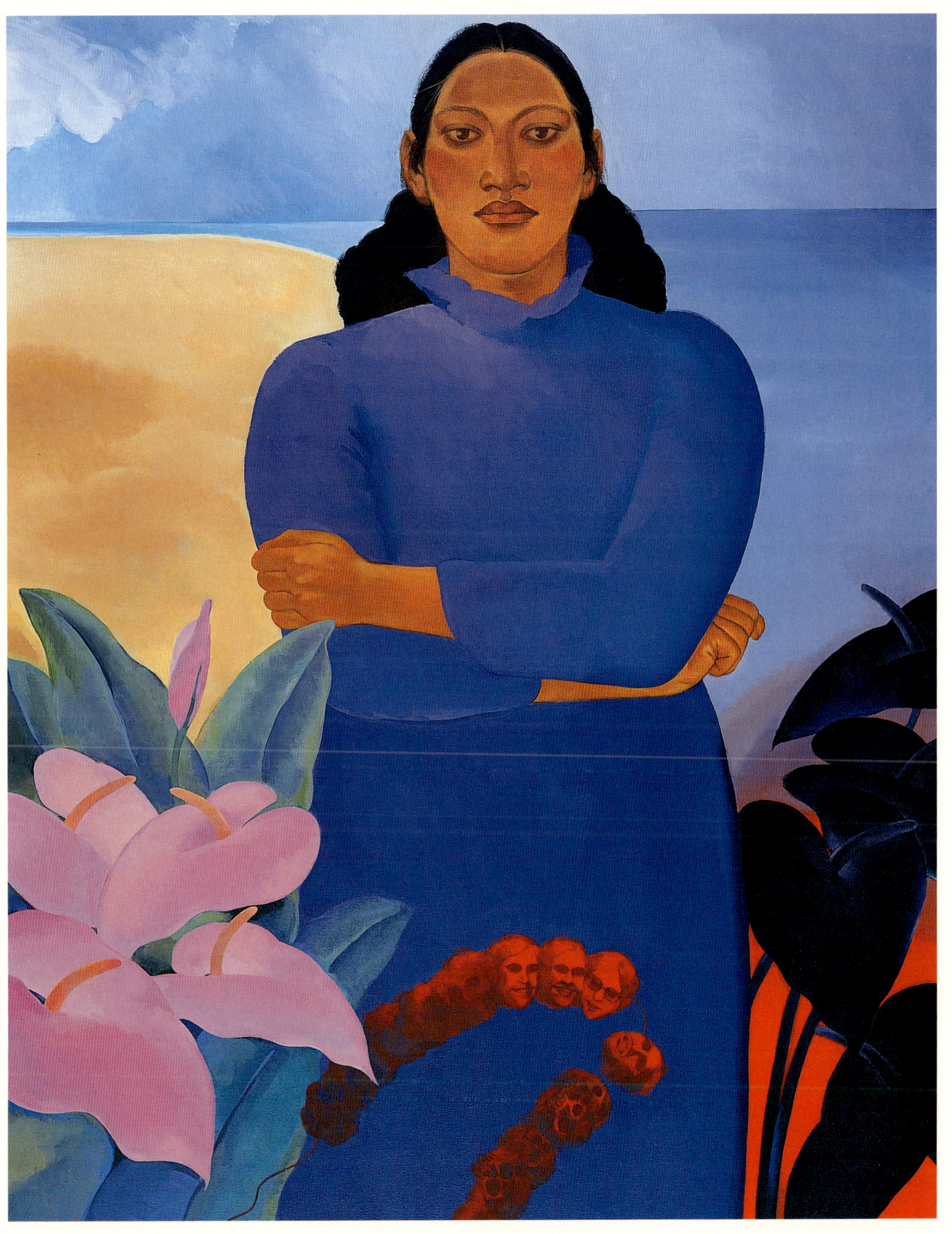

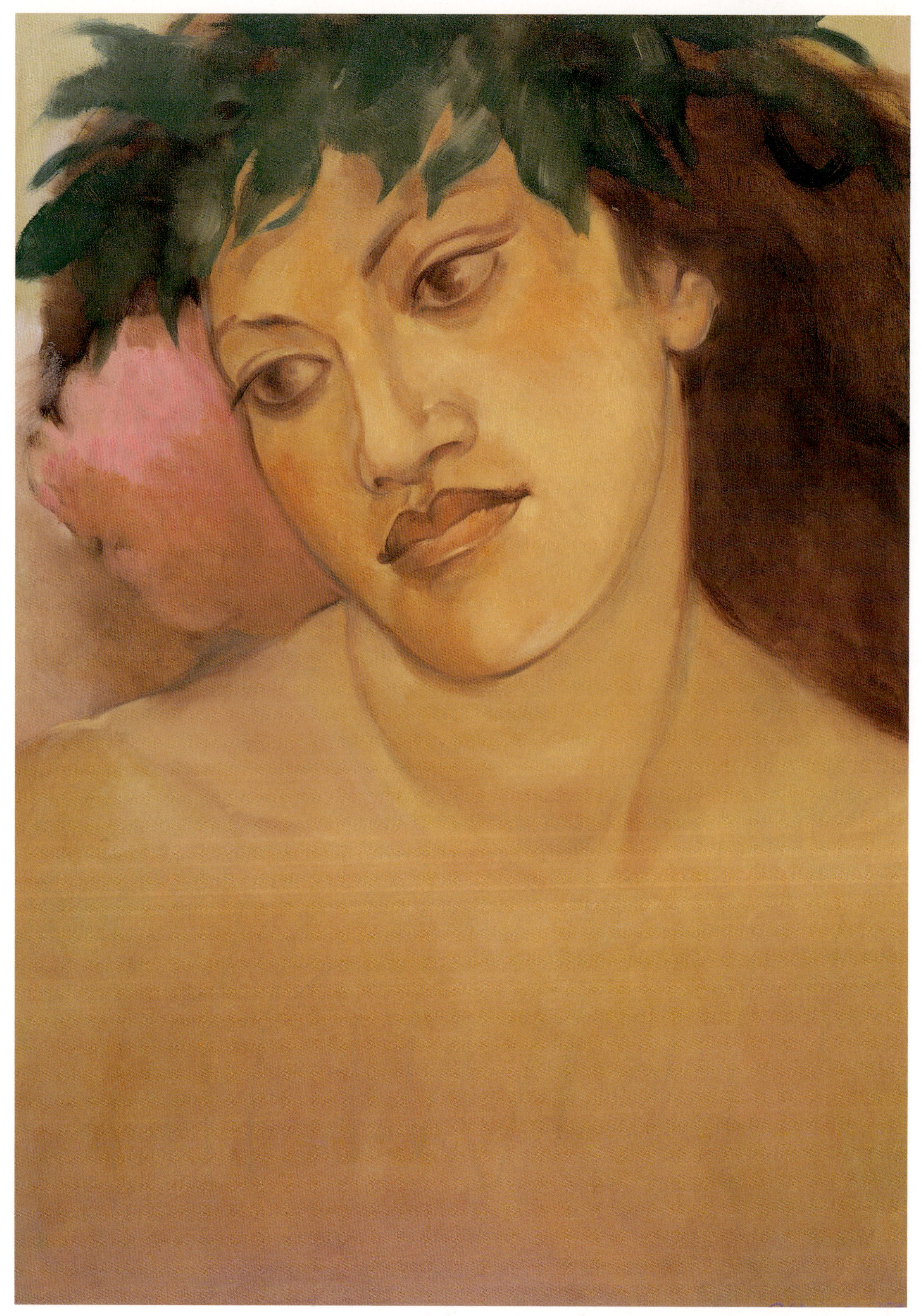